*Give Your Life
a Lift*

Give Your Life a Lift

Devotions in the Form of Modern Parables

HERMAN W. GOCKEL

CONCORDIA PUBLISHING HOUSE

St. Louis   London

Concordia Publishing House, St. Louis, Missouri
Concordia Publishing House Ltd., London, E. C. 1
© 1968 Concordia Publishing House
Library of Congress Catalog Card No. 68-20262

MANUFACTURED IN THE UNITED STATES OF AMERICA

4 5 6 7 8 9 10   99 98 97 96 95 94 93

Contents

Preface

*T*hese devotional units are in the form of modern parables. There is something about a parable that arrests our attention, holds our interest, and (at least in the parables that have come to us from the lips of our divine Lord) something that gives us a vivid insight into sacred truth which, in many cases, could have come to us in no other way.

That is why the Savior often expressed the profound thoughts of His message in simple narratives. He clothed His thoughts in flesh and blood and made them visual. To explain God's attitude toward His lost and straying children, for instance, He delivered no formal theological dissertation, but He told three short stories in quick succession: the stories of the lost sheep, the lost coin, and the lost son. (Luke 15)

Indeed, anyone who reads the four gospels is sure to remember the Master Teacher and Master Evangelist as the *Master Storyteller.* "Without a story spake He not to them . . . and the common people heard Him gladly."

This approach the author has sought to follow in these devotional readings. He makes no claim to originality for all illustrations used. Many have been culled from his reading. For these he wishes to give credit to their original authors. Some have been adapted or modified to suit his specific purpose. Others are original, based on personal observation or experience.

A topical index in the back of this volume will help the reader select devotional readings best suited to his specific needs and circumstances. The index will also help the layman, Sunday school teacher, or clergyman find an apt illustration for his purpose. It is the author's prayer that as the reader journeys through these pages he will gain fresh insights into the marvelous love of God as it has been revealed to us in Jesus Christ, His Son.

HERMAN W. GOCKEL

A Lift Along the Way

We have never been in India, but we are told that along the winding roads, especially in the hill countries, there are little resting places for travelers.

These are called *samatanga*. Here one may rest his weary feet, lay down his burden, and pause awhile to talk with other travelers. After a few moments of rest and mutual encouragement the traveler resumes his journey refreshed and strengthened.

It is not surprising, therefore, that many Christians in India have become accustomed to saying: "Christ is my Samatanga." For that is exactly what He is to the heart of the believer — a place of rest for the weary pilgrim, a place where burdens are laid down for the moment, a place from which one resumes his journey with a lighter heart and quickened step.

It may seem utterly incongruous and anachronistic to picture the inviting Christ standing as our Samatanga at the busy intersections of our modern cities or on the shoulders of our crowded freeways, inviting us to break our hectic pace for just a moment in order that we might be spiritually refreshed and strengthened.

Yet in a very real sense He is there, right in the midst of the daily grind. And He is still inviting: "Come unto Me, all ye that labor and are heavy laden, and I will give you *rest.* Take My yoke upon you, and learn of Me; for I am meek and

lowly in heart; and ye shall find *rest* for your souls."
(Matt. 11:28)

Is our heart heavy because of the recent loss of a loved
one? Have we been struggling with personal or family problems that defy solution? Has the Lord in His unsearchable
providence laid a cross upon our shoulders that is almost too
heavy for us to bear? Is the stretch of our journey that lies immediately ahead too difficult, too arduous, too frightening for
us to contemplate? Is our burden of sin and guilt too heavy
for us to bear?

Remember — we have a samatanga, a resting place along
our pilgrim path. Do we always take advantage of this resting
place? Do we really *unburden* ourselves to Him who has of-
fered to share our burdens? (1 Peter 5:7). Do we speak to
Him about our innermost fears and worries? Above all, do we
listen to Him when He assures us in the pages of His Word
that He will be with us always — with His gracious and sustaining and *forgiving* presence?

The poet Horatius Bonar knew Christ to be his Samatanga. Millions of Christians down through the years have
thanked this well-known hymn writer for putting his personal
experience into the familiar words:

> I heard the voice of Jesus say,
> "Come unto Me and rest;
> Lay down, thou weary one, lay down
> Thy head upon My breast."
> I came to Jesus as I was,
> Weary and worn and sad;
> I found in Him a *resting place,*
> And He has made me glad.

"In Thy Light"

A schoolteacher was taking her sixth-graders on a trip through the city art museum. At one point she noticed a group of three or four girls standing puzzled and bewildered in front of a beautiful oil painting that hung framed on the museum wall.

The girls were standing very close to the painting, and it was evident that they were not enjoying the work of art before them.

"Come over *here,* girls," the teacher called. *"This* is the point from which the painter wanted you to look at his work."

And from the middle of the large museum room, a good distance from the painting itself, the girls saw a beautiful landscape they had completely missed when standing close up.

Frequently in the midst of life, when we are surrounded by problems and perplexities that call for immediate solutions, we shall do well to heed the call of our Savior: "Come over *here,* My son, My daughter. *This* is the point from which your heavenly Father wants you to view your present circumstance."

As Christians we are to lead our entire lives, every moment of each day, in the perspective of eternity. We are, so to speak, to find a point of vantage outside our earthly pilgrimage. We are to stand in the very presence of our heavenly Father and look back with Him — as if looking from a mountaintop down into a verdant valley.

From there we will see that the road we are traveling,

though steep and difficult at present, leads surely to our Father's house.

The psalmist expressed this thought most beautifully when he said: "In Thy light shall we see light" (Ps. 36:9). The light of our puny reason is dim. It cannot reveal to us the entire landscape God has painted for our lives.

But in His light, the light that encompasses all eternity, we shall see the masterpiece He has planned — even for *our* lives — the masterpiece made possible by the glorious redemption that is ours through Jesus Christ, our Lord. The masterpiece which, when we see it from His perspective, includes both you and me forever happy in the mansions of His Father.

In the midst of life, when we are struggling with what seem to be almost insurmountable problems, especially when we are struggling with them close up, let us pray for the grace to see our problems in *His* light.

> Blind unbelief is sure to err
> And scan His work in vain;
> God is His own interpreter,
> And He will make it plain.

Love Is the Final Word

*T*here is a legend about the apostle John which, while it cannot be verified, is nevertheless very much in keeping with his character.

It is said that during his final years he lived in the city of Ephesus. Too old and too feeble to address a congregation with a formal sermon, he was nevertheless called upon to say a word to the worshipers at the close of every service.

Rising slowly, he would smile at the gathered group and with a quavering voice speak only one sentence: "Little children, love one another." And with that he would slowly seat himself again.

When one of his young friends asked him one day why he always said the same thing, he replied: "Because there is nothing more to say. That is the final word. If we love one another, that is everything."

How badly our bruised and bleeding world stands in need of this heavenly insight of the aged apostle! Yes, how badly you and I stand in need of it! In a day of short tempers, frayed nerves, and angry outbursts; in a day of petty jealousy, petty bickering, and petty backbiting; in a day when racial prejudice is filling men's hearts with unreasoning fear, hostility, and hatred — how important that we give ear to the aged apostle's plea: "Little children, *love* one another"!

Nor was he speaking of a merely sentimental love. The love of which he spoke was a love that was rooted in God. A theological love! How often he made this clear in his epistles!

14

"Beloved, let us love one another, for love is of God," he writes. "In this was manifested the love of God toward us, because that God sent His only-begotten Son into the world that we might live through Him. Herein is love, not that *we* loved God but that *He* loved *us* and sent His Son to be the Propitiation for our sins. Beloved, if God so loved us, we ought also to love one another." (1 John 4:7, 9-11)

The aged apostle, who in his youth had stood at the foot of the cross and had beheld the miracle of love, knew that you and I would have to go back to that same cross again and again, there to have our hearts emptied of hate and filled with love.

It was on Calvary that God spoke the final word — the word of love. With our eyes fixed on Him "who loved us and gave Himself for us," we must respond in the language of John: "If God so loved us, we ought also to love one another."

Just as You Are

A most interesting story is told of an Italian painter. One day he set out to walk the streets of his native city, searching for a man to serve as a model for a costly painting he was planning.

Late in the day he came upon an unshaven, ragged beggar. Here was the man he wanted! He gave him a sum of money and told him to report to his studio the first thing in the morning.

When the beggar appeared the following day, he was a different man — clean-shaven and neatly dressed! As a result he *lost* the privilege of sitting as the model for the painting.

The artist had wanted the beggar just as he was, unshaven and unkempt.

The analogy may be imperfect. Yet it does illustrate a basic truth of the Christian Gospel. Our Lord wants us to come to Him just as we are, not as we think we *should* be. To the Pharisees of His day Jesus said: "I am not come to call the righteous but sinners to repentance." (Matt. 9:13)

To Zacchaeus, the sinner who thought himself unworthy of the Savior's presence, He said: "The Son of Man is come to seek and to save that which was *lost*" (Luke 19:10). It was the spiritual beggar, the spiritual outcast, who was the object of His search.

Perhaps one of the most beautiful invitations recorded in the gospels are the well-known words of Christ: "Come unto

Me, all ye that labor and are heavy laden, and I will give you rest." (Matt. 11:28)

Did you notice to whom His invitation is addressed? All ye who are morally perfect? All ye who are paragons of piety? All ye who live in the suburbs? All ye who belong to the socially elite? All ye who serve on church committees? All ye who are pastors, professors, or Ph. D's?

No! "All ye that labor and are heavy laden." The offer of divine pardon, divine peace, and eternal rest in the mansions of His Father is made to those who are laboring under the burden of sin and are weighted down by the numberless and anonymous crosses of life.

"Come unto Me," He says to the spiritually hungry, the spiritually thirsty, the spiritually weary, the spiritually impoverished, "and I will give you rest" — the rest of full and free forgiveness, of sonship in His Father's family.

Yes, the gracious Lord of our salvation does want us (still wants us!) just as we are. Therefore—

> Let not conscience make you linger,
> Nor of fitness fondly dream;
> All the fitness He requires
> Is to feel your *need* of Him.

"Only One of Each of Us"

*T*he Sunday school teacher had ended her Bible story and was asking questions of her primary tots.

"Why, do you think, does God love us all so very much?" she asked.

There was momentary silence as the children wrinkled their little brows and "thought hard" for the proper answer. "Why does God love us — so very much?"

Suddenly little Kristin's hand shot up. And without the slightest doubt about the correctness of her answer she blurted: "Because He has only one of each of us."

Only one of each of us!

How true! And yet how seldom we reflect upon this precious thought! The great God of heaven who owns the sun, the moon, the stars, and the rolling spheres of the trackless universe has only *one* of you — and *one* of me. We are indescribably precious in His sight.

Again and again the Bible is at great pains to point out that God is concerned about you and me as individuals — as unique creations upon whom He is eager to lavish the fullness of His love. Perhaps best known are the reassuring words of Christ Himself: "Are not two sparrows sold for a farthing? And *one* of them shall not fall on the ground without your Father. But the very hairs of your head are numbered. Fear ye not therefore; ye are of more value than many sparrows." (Matt. 10:29-31)

And then there are God's extremely personal words spoken

18

through the prophet Isaiah: "Behold, I have graven thee upon the palms of My hands" (Is. 49:16). Behind that beautiful imagery lies the immovable assurance that you and I are as close to the heavenly Father, as dear to Him, as much the object of His daily attention and concern as if our faces had been inscribed on the palms of His omnipotent hands.

The God whom the Bible reveals does not only love the world in general, not only the great unnumbered masses who comprise the total human family. He knows and loves and cares for each single, solitary soul that issues forth from His creative hand.

You and I, who have been brought to faith in the Christian Gospel, can not only point to Christ and say: "He died for the sins of all the world." We can also point to Him and say: "He loved *me* and gave Himself for *me*." (Gal. 2:20)

Me — of whom He has only one!

Only Through the Cross

*T*here is a church in New York City whose front doors are most unusual. When the doors are closed, their ornately beveled panels form a beautiful cross. When the doors are opened, the cross divides, and the worshiper or visitor can walk right through the severed panels, down the center aisle of the nave, directly to the altar.

The designer had a simple explanation for the symbolism of these unusual doors. "It is only through the cross," he said, "that a man can step into the presence of a just and holy God." And so Sunday after Sunday it is through the severed arms of a wooden cross that the members of the congregation step out of the hubbub of their workaday world and into the presence of the Lord Most High.

In a sense that is what you and I do every day of our lives. We step into the presence of our God in prayer, in worship, and in praise, not in our own right but pleading the merits of His Son, who died for us on Calvary's cross. We can stand in the presence of the Lord of heaven only because His Son has made peace — peace between God and man — "by the blood of His cross." (Col. 1:20)

"The middle wall of partition," which had shut you and me out from the presence of our Maker, has been "broken down" because a complete reconciliation has been established "by the cross" of His beloved Son (Eph. 2:14-16). The Bible leaves no doubt that it is through the cross of Christ, through

His substitutionary death in our behalf, that we have gained entrance to the court of heaven.

In one of the most beautiful assurances of Holy Scripture we read: "Christ was delivered for our offenses and was raised again for our justification. *Therefore* . . . we have peace with God through our Lord Jesus Christ, by whom also we have *access* by faith into this grace wherein we stand." (Rom. 4:25 to 5:2)

It is through Christ, and through Him alone, that we gain entrance to the storehouse of spiritual treasures that a gracious God in heaven has prepared for us: forgiveness of sins, peace of soul, strength in the hour of trial, and the gilt-edged assurance of eternal bliss and glory. "I am the Door," the Savior once said. "*By Me* if any man enter in, he shall be saved." (John 10:9)

Yes, there is only one way, one door, one Savior by whom we can enter into the presence of the God of heaven. That way, that door, that Savior is Jesus Christ, our Lord, who died for us and rose again.

> Thou art the Way; to Thee alone
> From sin and death we flee;
> And he who would the Father seek
> Must seek Him, Lord, by Thee.

"I've Never Lived This Day Before"

*T*he elevator boy gave the white-haired man a cheery smile as he stepped into the elevator. It was early in the morning, and the elderly gentleman was his very first passenger.

Up and up the elevator soared, and as it did, the lad continued to whistle a merry tune. "Why so happy?" the dignified man inquired. Stopping his whistling just long enough to form his words, the bright-eyed lad replied: "I've never lived this day before!"

If only each of us could greet the dawn of each new day with the same wisdom, the same exuberance, the same eager spirit of adventure! Each day, as it comes to us fresh from the hand of God, is a *new* day — a day indeed that we have never lived before.

Let us live its 24 golden hours to the glory of Him to whom they belong. As we go forth to the tasks of each new morning, let us catch the spirit of the psalmist who exclaimed: "This is the day which the *Lord* hath made; we will rejoice and be glad in it" (Ps. 118:24). It is *His* day, but it is ours to use — for Him.

It is folly to carry the doubts, the disappointments, the troubles, the tears, the sin, the guilt of yesterday into the fresh, clean air of today. Our gracious Father in heaven is eager to erase them. His compassions fail not. They are new every morning. Great is His faithfulness. (Lam. 3:22)

Nor need we cast a pall of gloom across the brightness of today by borrowing the dark anxieties of tomorrow. Our Lord

22

will be in all of our tomorrows just as He has promised to be in all of our todays. And He will apportion to us the needed faith for every future moment. "As thy days, so shall thy strength be." (Deut. 33:25)

At the dawn of each new sun let us rejoice and be glad. For it is one of *God's* new days that is dawning — a day we have never lived before!

Lord, for tomorrow and its needs I do not pray,
Keep me, my God, from stain of sin *just for today.*
Let me both diligently work and duly pray;
Let me be kind in word and deed *just for today.*
Let me in season, Lord, be grave, in season gay;
Let me be faithful to Thy grace *just for today.*

"The Heavens Declare . . ."

A family was on its way to a Sunday outing in the mountains. It was midmorning when they drove by a church. Worshipers, dressed in their Sunday best, were seen gathered at the front entrance.

From the back seat of the car came the voice of 5-year-old Karen: "Daddy, aren't we going to go to church today?"

In the front seat both father and mother exchanged embarrassed glances. Since the question had been addressed to him, the father felt obliged to answer.

"We can worship God in the mountains," was his short reply. There was a brief moment of silence. Then from the back seat came the sage observation of which only a 5-year-old is capable: "But we *won't,* Daddy, *will* we?"

The father had sought refuge behind an evasion all too popular today, even among church members. It is true that our Lord can be worshiped in the mountains. He can be worshiped in the plains, in the valleys, and along a thousand streams. He can be worshiped anywhere.

But in her five short years Karen had learned that while God *can* be worshiped from hills or dales or mountaintops, He usually *isn't.*

The heavens may declare the glory of God, and the firmament may show His handiwork; but those who say they can worship God in the great outdoors seldom see the glory of God in the azure-blue heavens, nor do they see His handiwork in the firmament above.

More often than not they see the wonders of creation without giving thanks to the Creator who stands behind them all. And more often than not there is no mention at all of Him without whom there can be no Christian worship — the name above all other names, the blessed name of Jesus. (Phil. 2:9-10)

The majestic mountains may tell us of God's might, the surging rush of a waterfall may tell us of His power, the rolling spheres in the vaulted heavens may tell us of His wisdom, but only the Gospel of Jesus Christ can tell us of His saving love. And it is of this love that Christians sing in strains of joyful worship.

On mountaintops, in plains and valleys, beside the bubbling brooks the Christian heart can sing:

> Beautiful Savior,
> King of Creation,
> Son of God and Son of Man!
> Truly I'd love Thee,
> Truly I'd serve Thee,
> Light of my soul, my Joy, my Crown.
>
> Fair are the meadows,
> Fair are the woodlands,
> Robed in flowers of blooming spring;
> Jesus is fairer,
> Jesus is purer;
> He makes our sorr'wing spirit sing.

Our Dwelling Place

*T*he early evening storm had subsided, and the young father was putting his 5-year-old daughter Linda to bed for the night.

She had just finished her prayers. But no sooner had she spoken her final "amen" than she asked hurriedly and in a tone that betrayed her childlike worry: "Daddy, did you live in this house before I was born?"

"Yes, dear," he replied as he bent over to tuck her in snugly. "And did Grandpa live in this house before *you* were born?" Again he replied with a quiet yes.

There being no further questions, he gently kissed her forehead, bade her good night, and began to leave the room. But as he reached the door, he paused thoughtfully, then turned and inquired: "Why — why did you ask if Grandpa and I lived here before you came?"

"Oh, I was just thinking — if this house has been here that long, I don't have to be afraid when the wind blows."

Little Linda didn't know it, but many years ago a very great man found comfort in a thought very similar to hers. He, too, had lived through some frightening storms. And as he pondered the past and contemplated the future, he found his ultimate assurance in a remembrance very much like hers: "Lord, *Thou* hast been our dwelling place in all generations. Before the mountains were brought forth or ever Thou hadst formed the earth and the world, even from everlasting to everlasting Thou art God. (Ps. 90:1-2)

The psalmist had found his security in a "dwelling place"

that had existed long before he was born and would continue to exist long after he was gone — in the omnipotent God of heaven. As long as he could live *in Him,* he knew he was safe from every wind and tempest.

So, too, you and I. By faith in Christ we have found our dwelling place in Him who is eternal. And now, the Scriptures tell us, our lives "are hid with Christ in God" (Col. 3:3). In Him no evil can come near us.

What a splendid thought — at the dawn of each new day or the dawn of each new year — those words of little Linda! If the eternal God in whom we live and move and have our being has been here *that long,* we need not fear, whatever storms the coming day or the coming year may hold.

The Profoundest Thought of All

*T*he renowned theologian, Dr. Karl Barth, was spending an evening within the intimate circle of friends. Curious to know more about the great theologian's thinking, one of those present asked him: "What is the most profound thought that ever entered your mind?"

After a brief moment of reflection Dr. Barth replied very simply: "The most profound thought I have ever known is the simple truth: 'Jesus loves me, this I know, for the Bible tells me so.'"

To many this may not seem to be a profound thought at all. It may seem to be no more than a trite little ditty suitable for a beginners' class in Sunday school. But the glorious fact remains that no profounder thought has ever entered the heart of man than "Jesus loves me, this I know, for the Bible tells me so."

The apostle Paul devotes much of the first and second chapters of his first letter to the Corinthians to the "simplicity" of the Gospel message. Most of those who had embraced the Christian faith, he points out, were not among the so-called intellectuals or the socially elite but rather among the common, ordinary citizenry.

To them God had revealed what the "wise of this world" had failed to grasp: the essential meaning of the cross. To them God had revealed not only the message of His love in Christ but also the peace and the joy and the ultimate triumph which enter the hearts of all who believe.

It is in this connection that he exults: "Eye hath not seen nor ear heard, neither have entered into the heart of man the things which God hath prepared for them that love Him. But God hath revealed them unto us by His Spirit." (1 Cor. 2: 9-10)

The profoundest insights that have ever entered the heart of man are those that issue from the cross of Christ. Here we meet a God of love, a God of mercy, a God of infinite compassion, a God who redeems, forgives, restores for Jesus' sake, a God whom we can find *nowhere* else but in the "simple" Gospel of our Lord.

Whether we are a learned theologian or a bright-eyed child in Sunday school, it will remain forever true: The most profound thought we have ever had is the simple truth, "Jesus loves me, this I know, for the Bible tells me so."

Thank God for that!

Jesus Christ Is Not on Trial

*I*t was a weekday afternoon, and not many people were in the art gallery. As a result the middle-aged woman who had come to the gallery that day had almost the full-time attention of the curator, who was kind enough to explain the various paintings to her.

As she stood in front of a noted work of art, she began to voice her criticism of the craftsmanship of the artist. There was this and that about the painting that might have been improved. The curator listened patiently for a moment and then said gently: "Madam, in this gallery it is not the *artist* who is on trial — it is the *viewer*."

Her failure to appreciate or to be inspired by the masterpiece before her had much more to say about her than it did about the artist who had painted it.

It was not *he* who had been weighed and found wanting, but *she*.

How much the same is every man's encounter with Jesus Christ, the Savior! Men may presume to sit in judgment on the Man of Nazareth, they may cast doubt upon His deity, they may try to empty Him of His saviorhood, they may deny His glorious resurrection, they may try to rob His Gospel of its power and glory, but in the end it is always they, not He, who are judged.

His credentials have been established beyond doubt — Son of God and Son of Man, King of kings and Lord of lords, the same yesterday and today and forever. Of Him the Scriptures say: "He was declared to be the Son of God with power . . . by the resurrection from the dead." (Rom. 1:4)

Perhaps the most impressive and most eloquent listing of Christ's credentials is given us in the first chapter of Colossians. There we are told: "He is the Image of the invisible God, the Firstborn of all creation; for in Him all things were created, in heaven and on earth, visible and invisible, whether thrones or dominions or principalities or authorities — all things were created through Him and for Him. He is before all things, and in Him all things hold together . . . *that in everything He might be preeminent.*" (Col. 1:15-18 RSV)

Men may try to measure this Man of Galilee by human standards, but in the process it is *they* who are being measured. It is always they who are the smaller for the effort. Christ is not on trial. It is rather they who would presume to sit in judgment on Him who are on trial.

As for us, let us take our place with the saints of all ages and join daily in the triumph song:

> All hail the power of Jesus' name!
> Let angels prostrate fall;
> Bring forth the royal diadem
> And crown Him Lord of all.

"If Our Heart Condemn Us . . ."

A guilt-ridden young woman had confessed a terrible sin to her pastor.

Despite his best efforts to console her with the assurance of God's mercy and tender kindness, she sobbed: "But, Pastor, I just *know* I'm lost. God can *never* forgive the awful thing I've done."

The pastor thought a moment, then opened his Bible to a passage he had underscored many years before, a passage to which he himself had often fled in moments of doubt and faithlessness.

Handing her his Bible, he said: "Here, read the words I've underlined." Haltingly, between suppressed sobs, she read: "If our heart condemn us, God is greater than our heart and knoweth all things." (1 John 3:20)

What an unspeakably comforting assurance! Though our heart condemn us a thousand times, though it never cease to shout its endless accusations, "God is *greater* than our heart and knoweth all things."

But what is it that God knows — that can reverse the terrible judgment of our heart? What is it that God knows — that our deceitful heart has failed to tell us?

Right here is the indescribable wonder of the Christian faith. God looks at us through *Christ*. He knows, to be sure, that we are sinners; but He also knows that in Christ our guilt has been atoned, that in Christ our sins have been washed away, that in Christ we are completely righteous in His sight.

God *know*s these things, and there is never a moment when He does *not* know them. Our heart may forget, but God knows. Just as a passing storm cloud may blot out the sun for a moment and enshroud our little world in heavy darkness but can never remove the sun from the skies above us, so our little moments of doubt and despair can never erase the sun of God's mercy from the firmament of His promises.

Our heart, forgetful of His mercy, may confront us with the claims of God's consuming justice. But God, ever mindful of His Son's redeeming work for you and me, confronts us with the sweet assurance: "Son, be of good cheer; thy sins be forgiven thee." (Matt. 9:2)

Therefore, let all that is within me tell me that I am lost! It matters not. The source of my assurance rests in His all-knowing love. The anchor of my soul has found its hold in the eternal Rock of Ages. He is "greater than my heart." He knows all things, and *He* tells me I am saved.

"Underneath Are the Everlasting Arms"

*T*he story is told of a mother eagle that had built her nest on a ledge of rock jutting precariously over a steep and dangerous precipice.

Soaring through the air one day, returning to her nest, she was startled by what she saw. Clinging desperately to the jagged edge of a rock at the top of the canyon was her baby eagle, struggling with all its might to prevent a fall that was sure to crush its body more than a thousand feet below.

Unable to get to the ledge before her little one would fall, the mother eagle with the speed of lightning swooped low beneath the jutting rock, spread her strong wings to break the fall of her darling, and with her precious cargo clinging to the feathers of her mighty wings glided safely to the canyon's floor.

It was a picture similar to this that Moses had in mind when he assured the believers of his day: "The eternal God is thy Refuge, and *underneath are the everlasting arms.*" (Deut. 33:27)

As the mother eagle spread her strong wings to break the fall of her young one and then, on her extended wings, carried it to safety, so the eternal God stretches His "everlasting arms" underneath His frail and fragile children and protects their lives from danger.

How often, in days of illness or bereavement, in days of disappointment or disillusionment, in days of despair or perplexity, in days of loneliness or sorrow — when it seemed that every earthly prop had given way — have we been comforted and strengthened by the assurance that the eternal God is our Refuge and underneath are His everlasting arms!

His promise to all who put their trust in His eternal Son remains unbroken: "Fear thou not, for I am with thee. Be not dismayed, for I am thy God. I will strengthen thee; yea, I will help thee; yea, I will *uphold* thee with the right hand of My righteousness." (Is. 41:10)

In His promise we may rest secure.

> I am trusting Thee, Lord Jesus;
> Never let me fall.
> I am trusting Thee forever
> And for all.
>
> I am trusting Thee for power;
> Thine can never fail.
> Words which Thou Thyself shalt give me
> Must prevail.

The Waiting Father

A group of pastors had gathered for an informal evening. As frequently happens when clergymen get together, the conversation drifted to the subject of next Sunday's sermon. Two of the men were planning to preach on the Savior's well-known parable recorded in Luke 15:11-32.

Significantly, both men had chosen different themes for their sermons, although both were going to speak on the same text. The one said he was planning to preach on "The Prodigal Son," while the other announced that he was grouping his thoughts under the theme "The Waiting Father."

It is quite probable that both men preached excellent sermons on their differing themes, but somehow we incline to the opinion that the *second* man came closer to the purpose the Savior had in mind when He told this parable.

A reading of the entire chapter in which the parable of the lost son is told will indicate that the Savior's purpose in telling it was not so much to describe the behavior of the son as to describe the attitude of the father.

Luke 15 records three of the Savior's best-known picture stories. They are known as the parables of "the lost and found." He told the story of the lost sheep, not so much to describe the predicament of the sheep as to dramatize the solicitude of the man who owned it. He told the story of the lost coin, not so much to describe the plight of the coin as to show the deep concern of the woman who had lost it and her ceaseless efforts to recover it.

Similarly, He told the story of the lost son, not so much to impress us with the young man's lostness as to impress us with the love of his father — a love that remained warm and constant all the while the young man was wasting his substance in a far country, a love that impelled the father to welcome him back when he returned.

The main "characters" in these three stories were not the lost sheep, the lost coin, or the lost son, but the people who had *lost* them and who were desperately eager for their return. That is why we say that in all probability the clergyman who preached on "The Waiting Father" came closer to the Savior's intended purpose than the man who preached on "The Prodigal Son."

For ourselves, let us remember that it is not our sin but God's love that is the dominant theme of our lives. We have sinned, it is true. Sinned grievously! But the miraculous fact is that God loves us and forgives us — and restores us. We are all prodigal sons and daughters, it is true. But for us the tremendously important fact is that through Christ the God of heaven has become "The Waiting Father," waiting to receive us into our Father's house.

What a marvelously comforting assurance!

Letting the Light Shine Through

A little girl was among a group of people who were being conducted through a great cathedral. As the guide explained the various appointments, the little girl stood enthralled by a beautiful stained-glass window.

For a long moment she remained silent, looking up at the various figures in the window, her face bathed in a symphony of color as the afternoon sun poured into the transept of the huge cathedral.

As the group was about to move on, she gathered enough courage to address a question to the tour conductor. "Who are those people in the pretty window?" she asked. "Those, my child, are the saints," he replied.

That night, as the little girl was preparing to go to bed, she told her mother proudly: "I know who the saints are." "Oh?" replied the mother. "And just who *are* the saints?" Without a moment's hesitation the little one replied: "They are the people who let the light shine through!"

Her definition may never find its way into a dictionary, but this little tot gave voice to a truth that is both profound and Scriptural. God's saints *are* those through whom He chooses to shed His light upon this darkening world.

"You are a chosen race," He says, "a royal priesthood, a holy nation, God's own people, that you may declare the wonderful deeds of Him who called you out of darkness into His marvelous light." (1 Peter 2:9 RSV)

Like shafts of light that pierce the gathering gloom, the

wonderful deeds of God are to "shine through" the lives of His believers. Or in the Savior's words, His followers are to let their light so shine that men may see their good works and glorify their Father who is in heaven (Matt. 5:16). Through the good deeds of the believer the world is to see the Father.

The question for each of us to ask himself is: Am I letting God's light "shine through"? Can people see God — through me? Are His wonderful deeds reflected in my everyday behavior? Do those about me see in my attitudes, my words, my deeds a reflection of His love, His mercy, His tender kindness?

The Bible tells you and me that we are saints. Saints because of Christ. Saints because we have been washed clean in the blood of the Lamb. But as the saints of God, are we living up to our high and holy calling? Are we really "the people who let God's light shine through"? Pray God we are.

"The Right Side of Heaven"

*I*t was Christmas Eve. Six-year-old Mary Lou was walking down a dark city street with her father, on their way to the children's Christmas service.

Her active little mind was filled with the wonders of the event she and her classmates were about to celebrate — the coming of the Christ Child from heaven to earth, to be born a tiny infant in a lowly stable.

Above them was the velvety blue-black canopy of heaven, Swiss-dotted (as it seemed to her) with an infinite variety of brilliant lights twinkling down to earth.

Her eyes were fixed on the shimmering tapestry above as she and her father walked, silently but thoughtfully, toward the lighted church at the far end of the block.

Suddenly she looked up at her father and, with that rare insight peculiar to a 6-year-old, observed: "Daddy, I was just thinking — if the *wrong* side of heaven is so beautiful, how wonderful the *right* side must be!"

Little Mary Lou was right. No tongue or pen has ever succeeded in describing the glory, the grandeur, and the magnificence of our Father's house above.

That it is a place of entrancing beauty and matchless splendor the apostle John indicates in the Book of Revelation by describing heaven's glories in terms of costly jewels and precious gems and rarest metals.

How could heaven be anything else but beautiful! It is the habitation of our Lord, our compassionate and divine Redeemer, who left His home on high to dwell with us below. It is the royal palace of the King of kings.

And in that splendid palace — oh, wondrous thought! — the Son of God has gone ahead to prepare a place for those who trust Him as their Savior.

Through faith in His redeeming mercy they will ascend someday to His home beyond the skies — more exquisite, more glorious, more wonderful than human speech can tell.

Theologians may spin their theories as to whether or not Mary Lou's heaven is really a "place." But as she walked to church that Christmas Eve, Mary Lou had an insight which went far deeper than that of many a theologian.

It was the insight of childlike faith. To her heaven was where her Savior was. And for her that was a thought almost too wonderful for words.

More Time for Listening!

A busy preacher was telling a Quaker all the things he had to do during the coming week.

There were three sermons to deliver, two weddings to perform, two special addresses to be made, and nearly two dozen sick calls!

Raising his hand, the Quaker interrupted quietly and remarked dryly: "If thou doest so much talking, when hath the Lord a chance to talk to thee?"

A good question — not only for preachers and teachers but also for all who call themselves followers of the Lord Jesus Christ.

Of Jesus we are told that He frequently withdrew from the busy rounds of life to lonely mountain spots for quiet conversations with His Father. Even He needed the refreshment and encouragement that comes from quiet communion with heaven.

We read in Matthew: "And when He had sent the multitude away, He went up into a mountain apart to pray." In Luke we read: "He went out into a mountain to pray, and continued all night in prayer to God." In John we are told that after the feeding of the five thousand "He departed again into a mountain Himself alone."

And who will ever forget the scene in Gethsemane when, alone, He communed with His Father as the climax hour approached? We may be sure that not only did He *speak* during those sad and solitary moments, but He also *listened,* for He went forth from the Garden to carry out His Father's will.

How important that we follow His example! In our loud, confused, and topsy-turvy world in which each of us is on the go from morning to night, hurrying and scurrying from one appointment to another, how important that we *stop* at appointed intervals and cultivate the habit of quiet listening!

Before rising in the morning, at breakfast, on the way to work, at lunch, at dinner, upon retiring — there are countless opportunities throughout the day for closing the door against the noises of the world and for speaking and *listening* to our heavenly Father.

"In quietness . . . shall be your strength," the Lord told His people through the prophet Isaiah. If only each of us could cultivate more consistent habits of quietness — moments when our hearts and minds are attuned to our Lord and Savior!

Surely, many of us deserve the gentle rebuke of the Quaker: "If thou doest so much talking, when hath the Lord a chance to talk to thee?"

Prescriptions from Heaven

A pastor was visiting an elderly woman who had been chronically ill for many months. It was evident that her long confinement had resulted in a temporary period of melancholy which, despite her best efforts, she could not conceal from the man who had come to visit her.

Seated at her bedside, he said to her: "Now, if I were your doctor, you would expect me to write out a prescription and leave it with you. That is exactly what I am going to do." Taking a card from his pocket, he wrote on it the following words of Scripture: "Fear Thou not, for I am with thee; be not dismayed, for I am thy God. I will strengthen thee; yea, I will help thee; yea, I will uphold thee with the right hand of My righteousness." (Is. 41:10)

At the bottom of the card he wrote: "For use before retiring, upon awaking, and as often during the day as needed."

Have we ever thought of the Bible as God's pharmacy? Between its covers we can find prescriptions to meet our every need. In moments of depression it assures us of God's tender care. In moments of temptation it provides us with power to prevail. In moments of penitence it assures us of His love and mercy and His abundant pardon.

In the black night of dark despair it speaks to us from the heart of God: "Fear not, for I have redeemed thee. I have called thee by thy name. Thou art Mine. When thou passest through the waters, I shall be with thee; and through the rivers, they shall not overflow thee. . . . For I am the Lord, thy God." (Is. 43:1-3)

Have we stocked the shelves of our hearts with these prescriptions from heaven? Can we reach into the storehouse of our memory for just the right word at just the right time — for just the right word of comfort, correction, admonition, or encouragement?

Surely, we have every reason to pray the ancient collect: "Blessed Lord, who hast caused all Holy Scriptures to be written for our learning, grant that we may in such wise hear them, read, mark, learn, and inwardly digest them, that by patience and comfort of Thy holy Word we may embrace, and ever hold fast, the blessed hope of everlasting life, which Thou hast given us in our Savior Jesus Christ."

To those who "hear, read, mark, learn, and inwardly digest" the Holy Scriptures, they are indeed *filled* with "prescriptions from heaven."

Our Infinite God

One day St. Augustine, the great church father, was walking along the seashore in quiet meditation. His thoughts were centered on the doctrine of the Holy Trinity. How could God be three — and yet be one?

While wrestling with this baffling thought, his attention was suddenly drawn to a little girl playing in the sand. Back and forth she went, carrying a shell full of water from the receding waves to a little hole she had dug.

"What are you doing, little girl?" he asked. Without hesitation and with an air of childlike confidence she replied: "Oh, I'm going to empty the sea into this little hole I've dug."

The wise theologian smiled and resumed his walk. But as he strolled along the shore, he said to himself: "I am trying to do exactly what that little girl is doing — trying to crowd the infinite God into this finite mind of mine."

We may not be able to comprehend the doctrine of the Holy Trinity with our puny intellect, but we can believe what the Scriptures tell us about the God of our salvation. It is not so much a matter of comprehending as it is trusting.

We can trust that the grace of the Lord Jesus Christ (the Second Person of the Holy Trinity) and the love of God the Father (the First Person) and the communion of the Holy Ghost (the Third Person) will be with us always, keeping, guarding, and sustaining us. (2 Cor. 13:14)

The revelation of the Holy Trinity, given us in Scripture, is most comforting and reassuring. It tells us not only that there is a God in heaven who has made us, but also that this God has sent His only Son into the world to redeem us, and that through the power of His Holy Spirit He will keep us in the faith until the day of final judgment.

As we fold our hands in sleep each night, we can safely commit our bodies and souls to the Father, Son, and Holy Spirit — to the Father, who loved us and gave us His Son; to the Son, who loved us and gave His life that we might live; and to the Holy Spirit, who loved us and through the Gospel brought us to the God of our salvation.

Comprehend the great God of the universe with our pigmy intellect? No! No more than the little girl could encompass the ocean in the little hole she had dug. We need not comprehend! We need only to *commit* — to commit ourselves to the grace, the mercy, and the pardon He has promised.

"Make All the Good People Nice"

A young mother was putting her 5-year-old daughter to bed and was listening to her prayers.

It was their custom that after the child had said two or three formal prayers she would conclude by adding a childlike petition of her own.

After concluding her formal prayers on this particular evening, she paused for a moment and then added this thoughtful plea: "O God, make all the bad people good and all the good people nice."

We are not sure just what she meant by those final words, but we do have a pretty good idea. If only all the *good* people in the world were — *nice!* If only all who profess the Christian faith, who attend church, who work on committees, who represent the church to the world were as pleasant, as winsome, and as winning as Christ's followers ought to be!

All too frequently those who profess to be doing the work of the church (the good people!) carry on their work with a brusqueness, a lovelessness, and a nastiness that ill becomes a disciple of our Lord. In their own estimation they may indeed be good; but in the estimation of our little girl with the folded hands they surely aren't nice.

Yet our Lord expects His good people to be nice — pleasant, gentle, kind, and amiable. In the words of St. Paul, they are to "adorn the doctrine of God, our Savior, in all things" (Titus 2:10). Or as the New English Bible puts it, Christians are so to comport themselves in their everyday behavior that "they will add lustre to the doctrine of God our Savior."

By their attitude and by their actions they are to make the Christian Gospel more attractive to all with whom they come in contact.

Are we doing that? There is danger that even those who claim to know the joy of God's salvation present a sour visage to the world. That even those who claim to know the love of God repel their fellowmen with bitter words and cutting language. That even those who work most assiduously for the cause of Christ and for His church are most unpleasant to those with whom they live in closest contact.

Perhaps our little girl with the folded hands was thinking of *them* when she prayed: "O God, make all the bad people good and *all the good people nice!*"

Einstein — On Fourth World War

*T*he late Albert Einstein, during his declining years, granted a press conference to a number of newspaper reporters.

After they had plied him with questions on many subjects, one reporter asked: "Mr. Einstein, would you care to make a prediction as to the kind of weapons that will be used in the third world war?"

Modestly he shook his head and said: "No, I would not venture a prediction." After the briefest hesitation he added: "But I'll tell you what will be the chief weapon in the *fourth* world war."

The reporters were all ears, and every pencil was poised in anticipation of the old man's prediction. What *would* be the chief weapon in the fourth world war?

With an air of finality, the old man gave a one-word reply — clubs!

It took a moment or two for the aged scientist's reply to register, but as it did, a grim silence settled over the assembled group.

No one who scans the horizons of our world today can say that the future is anything but grim. Man's technology has so far outdistanced his morality that many are speaking of the end of civilization as we have known it.

There is a strange echo abroad in the land, the echo of the Savior's words, "Men's hearts failing them for fear and for looking after those things which are coming on the earth." (Luke 21:26)

What is to be the attitude of the believer in the face of this growing pessimism? He is to heed the word of the Lord as spoken through the prophet Jeremiah to the anguished Jewish exiles in the land of Babylon: "Seek the welfare of the city where I have sent you into exile, and pray to the Lord on its behalf, for in *its* welfare you will find *your* welfare" (Jer. 29:7 RSV). The believer is to pray, to work, to strive for the welfare of the world in which he is, admittedly, only a pilgrim.

The believer in Christ is part of the very world that is on the verge of destruction. It is up to him to seek the welfare of that world — by prayer, by work, by taking an ever greater hand in the affairs of men and nations. It is his world as much as theirs.

But in his heart of hearts he will always carry the unbreakable assurance of Him who has promised: "Lo, I am with you alway, even unto the end of the world" (Matt. 28:20). In *His* power the believer must ultimately prevail.

"But Now *Is* Christ Risen!"

*A*n honest doubter once asked a Christian pastor: "If it could be proved that Christ never rose from the grave — *what then?*"

The pastor thought a moment, looked his questioner squarely in the eye, and replied: "Then nineteen centuries of Christian preaching have been built upon a lie. Then the faith of millions has been in vain. Then all who believe in Christ today are still living, unforgiven, in their sins. Then those who have died trusting in Him have perished. Then the members of my congregation and Christian people everywhere are, of all men, most miserable."

Noticing that his doubting friend was astonished by the grimness of his reply as well as by its detailed completeness, the pastor continued: "You see, the question you just put to me was asked and answered some nineteen hundred years ago — in the pages of the Bible, in the fifteenth chapter of Paul's first letter to the Corinthians."

Going on to expound this glorious chapter of our resurrection faith, the pastor pointed out that it is not so much a question of "if Christ be not risen, what *then?*" It is rather a question of "since Christ *is* risen, what *now?*"

Now the message of victory over death which Christian pastors have been proclaiming for nineteen centuries has been authenticated, for the triumphant Christ was "declared to be the Son of God with power . . . by the resurrection from the dead." (Rom. 1:4)

Now the faith of millions down through the centuries has been given an immovable rock on which to rest, for "He was delivered for our offenses and was raised again for our justification." (Rom. 4:25)

Now all who put their trust in Him today can draw immeasurable comfort, courage, and strength from His words: "I am the Resurrection and the Life. He that believeth in Me, though he were dead, yet shall he live. And whosoever liveth and believeth in Me shall never die." (John 11:25-26)

Now all who are called upon to walk through the valley of the shadow of death can look forward confidently to the far side of the valley, because they know that their omnipotent, resurrected Lord can keep His promise to them: "Because I live, ye shall live also." (John 14:19)

Thank God, the question this Easter Sunday will not be: "If Christ be not risen, *what then?*" but rather: "Since Christ *is* risen, *what now?*"

And the answer will ring — clear, loud, exalted, and triumphant — from a million Christian voices:

> He lives triumphant from the grave,
> He lives eternally to save,
> He lives all-glorious in the sky,
> He lives exalted there on high.

God's Grace — Unlimited and Undeserved

*T*o most of us the name Copernicus conjures up only the thought of a famed astronomer — a mathemetician whose accomplishments changed man's conception of the universe. To be sure, he *was* that. But he was much more.

He was also a child of God who had learned to know and trust his Savior. When he was critically ill with his final illness, his book *On Revolutions of the Celestial Bodies,* just off the press, was laid in his arms.

But when the final moment drew near, he did not think of himself as an astronomer or a scientist but only as a sinner who needed the forgiveness of His Savior. He asked that the following epitaph be written on his gravestone:

"Lord, I do not ask the kindness Thou didst show to Peter. I do not dare to ask the grace Thou didst grant to Paul. But, Lord, the mercy Thou didst show to the dying robber, that mercy show to me. That earnestly I pray."

Surely you and I could think of no better prayer to offer to our Lord. When we measure ourselves against such great men as Peter or Paul or other outstanding servants of the Lord, we are in danger of thinking (falsely, of course!) that somehow they were more worthy of God's grace or kindness than we.

But when we think of the thief on the cross, with a misspent life behind him and imminent death before him, we know that he had nothing to offer his Lord but a repentant, trusting heart. And *that,* surely, you and I have, too.

Let our past be whatever it has been. Let our sins be "red like crimson." Let our record be one of repeated failure. Let our conscience clamor with endless accusations. Let our heart be filled with remorse and regret over "the sin which doth so easily beset us." Let these things all be so.

We still can pray the pleading prayer of humble Copernicus: "Lord, the mercy Thou didst show to the dying robber, that mercy show me. That earnestly I pray." Whether we realize it or not, the mercy that was shown the dying thief was the same mercy that was shown to Peter and Paul.

For it lies in the very nature of God's grace and mercy that it is entirely *undeserved.* Peter, Paul, the robber, you, and I — we all are dependent on the very same "kindness" of our Lord for the full forgiveness of our sins.

It is the divine kindness not only revealed by, but also made possible by, Jesus Christ, our Lord and our Redeemer, yes, *your* Lord and *your* Redeemer. Therefore —

> Let not conscience make you linger
> Nor of fitness fondly dream;
> All the fitness He requires
> Is to feel your *need* of Him.

The Art of Looking Up

A cartoon, appearing in a daily newspaper recently, preached an eloquent sermon.

It showed a crowd of people walking along a busy downtown street. Each person had his head slanted downward at the same angle, and each had his eyes fastened on the sidewalk.

At the bottom of the cartoon appeared the surprising legend (surprising, that is, for a large metropolitan daily): "Almost no one looks *up* any more."

How true! Modern man, crowded in by the forest of steel and concrete which he has built and in which he must carve out a living for himself and for his family, has lost the capacity to "look up."

For him there are no majestic mountain peaks that speak to him of the Eternal. No hills beyond whose distant crest there lies the promise of a new tomorrow. Nothing but sidewalks and pavements and asphalt and bricks and buildings.

What modern man needs, yes, what you and I need, is to break out of the suffocating walls with which we have surrounded our lives and to look *out* and look *up* to the panorama of God's promises. His promises are still there, as they have been "ever of old." They are there every morning.

King David, who had spent his youth tending sheep within sight of the Judean hills, learned that there was spiritual strength in looking up. Listen to the hymn of the shepherd-turned-king: "I will lift up mine eyes unto the hills, from whence cometh my help. My help cometh from the Lord, which made heaven and earth. He will not suffer thy foot to be moved; He that keepeth thee will not slumber. Behold, He that keepeth Israel shall neither slumber nor sleep. . . . The Lord shall preserve thee from every evil; He shall preserve thy soul. The Lord shall preserve thy going out and thy coming in from this time forth and even forevermore." (Ps. 121)

Such was the confidence of the man who had learned to lift his eyes to the mountains, knowing that *beyond* the mountains was the God of his salvation. "My help cometh from the Lord!"

You and I can do what David did. No matter where we are, no matter what our circumstance, we can raise our hearts heavenward each morning, noon, and night — "Looking unto Jesus, the Author and Finisher of our faith" (Heb. 12:2). He will not suffer our foot to be moved. He will preserve us from every evil.

Have we cultivated the art of looking up?

Still Members of the Church!

We are told that the ancient church had a custom that was both beautiful and meaningful.

When a member of the congregation died, his name was not removed from the membership list, but following his name a notation was added: "Transferred to the church above."

So sure were they of the unity of the church below and the church above that death was merely a transfer — merely a changing over, a moving from one congregation of saints to another. What a beautiful thought!

But the thought is more than beautiful — it happens to be true, as true as any other truth that God has given us in the pages of His Word. There is no reason why you and I cannot be just as sure of this glorious fact as were the believers of an earlier age.

Our loved ones who have departed this life, trusting in Christ as Savior and Lord, are still members of the church of which Christ is Head. They and we are still united in that "mystic sweet communion" which binds together all those who belong to Him.

St. Paul puts this comforting truth very clearly when he says: "If we live, we live to the Lord, and if we die, we die to the Lord; so then, whether we live or whether we die, *we are the Lord's*. For this end Christ died and lived again, that He might be Lord both of the dead and of the living." (Rom. 14:8-9 RSV)

Christ is still the living Lord of our departed loved ones. They are still members of His church. But they are now members of the church triumphant, the church of which the ancient seer spoke prophetically: "And the ransomed of the Lord shall return and come to Zion with songs of everlasting joy upon their heads; they shall obtain joy and gladness, and sorrow and sighing shall flee away." (Is. 35:10)

What an unspeakable comfort when we stand at the bier of a departed loved one to know that he and we are still members of *one* church, that we are still loved and held by the same Lord, that we still worship at the same throne, the throne of the Lamb that was slain and has won for us the victory!

We who remain behind, it is true, must worship the Lamb by faith. They who have gone on before, who have been *transferred,* are worshiping Him by sight. Someday when the clocks of heaven strike the hour for that great joint service which will never end they and we shall worship Him *together.*

Of the church on earth and the church above the hymn writer assures us:

> Yet she on earth hath union
>   With God the Three in One,
> And mystic sweet communion
>   With those whose rest is won;
> O happy ones and holy!
>   Lord, give us grace that we
> Like them, the meek and lowly,
>   On high may dwell with Thee.

The World of Rising Expectations?

*T*wo clergymen were seated in a living room, listening to a panel discussion on television. Again and again the discussants referred to our present world as "a world of rising expectations."

They pointed out how the have-not nations are clamoring to be numbered among the haves, how vast areas which only a generation ago were backward and primitive are surging forward by leaps and bounds, and how in our own country the impoverished and underprivileged are insisting on a proportionate share of the material wealth of our prosperous land.

These developments, they pointed out, were all part of an emerging pattern, all part of "a world of rising expectations."

After the program was over, the two clergymen engaged in a few moments of quiet and reflective conversation. In a sense they agreed with the men on the television panel: ours *is* a world of rising expectations. But in another sense they disagreed, and they expressed their regret and alarm.

"Ours is really a world of *lowered* expectations," said the one. "How often do we hear men speak, publicly or even in private, about the *ultimate* expectations of man? There was a day, for instance, when one could use the word 'heaven' in ordinary conversation and not expect a patronizing smile; now the very word in many cases invites the smirk of 'pie in the sky.'"

Indeed, in *this* sense ours is a world of lowered expectations. Many are no longer looking forward to those things for which the early Christians lived: the triumphant return of the Savior, the permanent release from this world's sorrows, and eternal life with Christ in never-ending bliss and glory.

To a world that finds its highest expectations in the products of an improved technology there can be little meaning in the well-known words of Paul: "We are citizens of heaven; our outlook goes beyond this world to the hopeful expectation of the Savior who will come from heaven, the Lord Jesus Christ." (Phil. 3:20 Phillips)

Yet these words are of the very essence of our Christian faith. Our citizenship *is* in heaven. Our highest expectation is to reach the homeland and to be with our Brother Christ. With Paul the heaven-oriented believer says: "I have a desire to depart and to be with Christ, which is far better" (Phil. 1:23). In his own way — that is, in the Scriptural way — the believer does live in a world of "rising expectations."

> Draw us to Thee,
> For then shall we
> Walk in Thy steps forever
> And hasten on
> Where Thou art gone
> To be with Thee, dear Savior.

"This *One* Thing I Know . . ."

A layman in the Bible was confronted by a serious theological problem. Blind from birth, he had spent all his days begging on the streets of Jerusalem.

The routine of his life was upset one day when Christ approached him and restored his sight. From that moment on he was hounded and persecuted by the church leaders of his day, who even dragged his parents into court for an open hearing.

The ecclesiastical authorities wanted the former blind man to make a public statement to the effect that the man who had healed him was not a prophet, nor was he even a member of the establishment, but just an ordinary sinner.

Worn down by cruel cross-examination, the poor man, who was no match for his clever interrogators, finally blurted: "Whether he be a sinner or no, I know not. But *one thing I know,* that, whereas I was blind, now I see." (John 9:25)

In those final words the former blind man has given us the quintessence of all effective Christian witnessing. Also the touchstone of all valid theological argumentation.

In effect, he was saying: "You may have all the clever arguments on your side. In fact, by your polished logic you may even end up 'proving' to me that the man who healed me was a sinner. But there's one thing you'll never be able to change, one thing on which you'll never be able to change my mind: I used to be blind, and now I see!"

Raised to the spiritual level, that was essentially the witness of the apostle Paul throughout the Book of Acts and all of his epistles. "I, the man who was totally blind, have been given sight!" What Christ had done for him, for him personally, was so evident, so incontrovertible, so unassailably true that he could stand before kings and say: "This one thing I *know!*"

So, too, can you and I. We may not be able to match wits with brilliant theologians, we may not be able to meet the professional philosopher on his own ground, but we can tell all and sundry: "Whether your impressive argumentation be right or wrong, I do not know. But this *one* thing I know, that, whereas I was blind, now I see."

And, like Paul, we can dedicate our lives, no matter how humble they may be, to the Man who gave us sight. Remember Paul's eloquent words? "I am crucified with Christ; nevertheless I live; yet not I, but Christ liveth in me. And the life which I now live in the flesh I live by the faith of the Son of God, who loved me and gave Himself for me." (Gal. 2:20)

> Thee we own a perfect Savior,
> Only Source of all that's good.
> Every grace and every favor
> Comes to us through Jesus' blood.
>
> Faith He grants us to believe it,
> Grateful hearts His love to prize;
> Want we wisdom? — He must give it:
> Hearing ears and seeing eyes.

Epitaph — In a Word

*A*lmost hidden in a secluded corner of a New York cemetery is a small gravestone polished smooth by the wind and weather of many years.

The stone bears no name, nor is there any date inscribed on it. To the stranger passing by it tells nothing about the man or the woman or the child whose final resting place it marks.

Nothing except one thing. Still legible on the face of the fading stone, in letters that neither wind nor weather has been able to erase, is one solitary word, the simple word "forgiven."

The nameless person lying there had rated no monument. No obelisk. No marble statuary in a vaulted mausoleum. No bronze plaque embossed with brilliant feats accomplished, splendid goals achieved, or heroic battles won.

Just a simple stone. And just a single word — *forgiven.*

Yet could any epitaph be more glorious? To have found forgiveness at the hand of a merciful God — could anything be more wondrous? To have been welcomed home by a gracious Father who is willing to forgive the sins of His prodigal children — could any life have ended in greater rapture?

At death's door, when all of life's vanities must be left behind, what word will calm our troubled spirit, if not the word *forgiven?*

Thank God, that thrilling word can be written as the epitaph of all His believers. Through Christ we have become God's forgiven children. St. John tells the believers of his day:

"I write unto you, little children, because your sins are forgiven you for His name's sake." (1 John 2:12)

This is the same beloved disciple who wrote: "The blood of Jesus Christ, His Son, cleanseth us from all sin. . . . If we confess our sins, He is faithful and just to *forgive* us our sins and to cleanse us from all unrighteousness." (1 John 1:7, 9)

What greater bliss, when we stand at the portals of eternity, than to know that our guilty record has been washed clean by the blood of Jesus Christ, our Savior! In Him we have forgiveness. (Eph. 1:7)

What more glorious, more victorious epitaph for you and me than the single word *forgiven*!

> Jesus, Thy blood and righteousness
> My beauty are, my glorious dress,
> Wherein before my God I'll stand
> When I shall reach the heavenly land.

The Art of Sermon Twisting

*T*he Sunday school teacher was just bringing her lesson on the Good Samaritan to a close. She had told her primary tots the story in great detail, making applications of the Savior's parable to the lives of her pupils as she went along.

When she was finished, she asked little Tommy what he had learned from the story of the Good Samaritan. He wrinkled his little forehead, thought hard, and then replied with an air of omniscience: "I have learned that when I get into trouble, somebody should help me out."

We can smile at Tommy's answer, but, on second thought, isn't there very much of you and me in his reply? Like many of us adults, the lad had listened to the whole story *only* from the viewpoint of his sinful, selfish heart.

The priest, the Levite, the Samaritan, and anyone else who journeyed down the Jericho road that day, all were supposed to help little Tommy. By a selfish twist of his little mind he had cast himself in the role of the man to be helped — not in the role of those who should help.

And who of us hasn't, on occasion, practiced the same nefarious art of sermon twisting? There is something demonic about the way we can misapply the evident truths of the Gospel message.

We can listen to a stirring sermon on the great hymn of love in First Corinthians 13 and then fold our hands over our hymnal thinking: What a wonderful world this would be if everyone (else?) would exercise the grace of Christian charity!

66

We can listen to eloquent addresses on social justice, racial equality, Christian fellowship, and human brotherhood — and then, by a logic dictated by our selfish heart, start counting the blessings that would accrue to us in a world in which all men were truly brothers.

Frequently, we must admit, our motivations are not much higher than those of little Tommy, who could listen to the story of the Good Samaritan and then say: "I have learned that when I get into trouble, somebody should help me out."

Both little Tommy and we must learn again and again (as self-evident as it may seem) that the Savior was speaking of the man who acted, the man who helped, when He said: "Go and do thou likewise!"

> May we Thy precepts, Lord, fulfill
> And do on earth our Father's will
> As angels do above;
> Still walk in Christ, the living Way,
> With all Thy children and obey
> The law of Christian love.

"Show Me the Church with the Cross"

*I*t was beginning to get dark on the streets of London, and the lights in the lampposts were just going on. A little girl who had lost her way stood crying on a street corner.

She was sobbing her heart out when a policeman found her. Trying to help her, he asked, "Do you live near a big building of any kind — a school, a fire house, a police station?" "No," she replied, she didn't.

"Do you live near a park? A playground?" "No," not by a park or playground either. "Well," the policeman went on, "do you live near a church?"

Suddenly the tear-streaked face lighted up. "Yes, I live by the church with the cross. Show me the church with the cross, and I'll know my way home."

Apocryphal or not, the story illustrates a profound theological truth. Sooner or later in the lives of all of us the lights begin to go out, the way grows dim, and we find ourselves bewildered and lost. The old familiar landmarks no longer point the way.

Answers that used to answer no longer answer. Solutions that used to solve no longer solve. The clear, clean windows through which we looked at a world of joy and beauty in the morning suddenly become a hall of mirrors reflecting images that are grotesque and ugly. And we are confused, bewildered, lost.

From such lostness there is only one direction in which

you and I can walk with safety and assurance. "Show me the church with the cross, and I'll know my way home."

Only in the message of God's all-redeeming love, revealed to you and me on Calvary's cross, can a confused humanity ultimately find its bearings. Only at the foot of the cross do the tangled and twisted highways and byways of life become straight and fall into place. Only at the foot of the cross does the way home, which was temporarily obscured, once more become clear.

That is why the apostle Paul was always and forever pointing his converts to the cross of the Savior whom he preached. To the Corinthians he wrote: "I determined not to know anything among you save Jesus Christ and Him crucified." (1 Cor. 2:2)

To the Galatians he wrote: "I am crucified with Christ. Nevertheless I live . . . and the life which I now live in the flesh I live by faith in the Son of God, who loved me and gave Himself for me." (Gal. 2:20)

To Paul the cross was the central fact of his faith, the central focus of his life. And so it must be for you and me. As the little girl in the gathering dusk on the streets of London, you and I can say: "Show me the church with the cross, and I'll know my way home."

Washington the Capital of Vermont!

*T*en-year-old Robert had not done his homework the night before. And so he struggled through his written test in geography, doing a lot more guessing than he should have.

All evening, as his mind went back to the written test and some of the answers he had given, he was deeply troubled. What if too many of his answers had been wrong? What if he would receive a failing grade?

That night, after he had said his prayers, he suddenly blurted the nervous postscript: "And, please, God, make Washington the capital of Vermont!"

You and I may not have been quite as naive as little Robert, but has not some of our praying been very much like his?

How often have we been flagrantly remiss in the performance of our duty and then have come to God in prayer, asking *Him* to do what we have failed to do — as if by the waving of some magic wand we could be absolved from what was clearly our solemn duty?

How often have we deliberately done those things which we knew we shouldn't and then have come running to our heavenly Father, asking Him to make right of our wrong?

Or, in the analogy of little Robert, how often have we in our negligence or folly said that Washington was the capital of Vermont and then (at least, in effect) have pleaded with our Father in heaven to make it so?

It is true, a gracious God in heaven has promised to forgive us our sins for Jesus' sake — yes *all* our sins — but this does not mean that He has absolved us from doing, right now, what is clearly our duty.

The privilege of prayer is neither a license to laziness nor an invitation to indolence. The praying Christian must still do his homework.

Martin Luther once said that we are to pray as if everything depended on God and then work as if everything depended on us. Prayer and work are not mutual exclusives. They are correlatives. They go hand in hand.

It is significant that among the books of the Bible which have the most references to prayer is the Book of *Acts.* The early Christians not only prayed, they acted. They lived out their prayers in their daily lives. They *lived* the way they *prayed.*

As you and I grow more and more in Christian grace and knowledge, we will have less and less need to pray the prayer of little Robert: "Please, God, make Washington the capital of Vermont!"

The Touch of the Master

A distinguished visitor was spending a few days with the late Albert Schweitzer in Africa. Upon entering the dining room the first evening, he saw a piano which he described as old, broken-down, and warped.

After the meal was finished, Dr. Schweitzer, as was his custom, sat at the keyboard of the decrepit instrument and began to play. Within a moment the room was filled with beautiful and majestic harmonies.

Describing the incident later, the visitor wrote into his diary: "The old piano seemed to *lose its poverty* in his hands." What an apt description of the spell of the master musician!

What an apt description, too, of the transforming power of the grace of God through Jesus Christ, our Lord! In His omnipotent and loving hands, old, broken-down, and sinful lives can "lose their poverty" and become rich with love and truth and beauty.

The human heart, the Bible tells us, is by nature desperately warped and twisted — capable of producing the ugliest of discord and disharmony. "Out of the heart," the Savior says, "proceed evil thoughts, murders, adulteries, fornications, thefts, false witness, blasphemies." (Matt. 15:19)

So abject is the spiritual poverty of the human heart that it can do nothing about its bankrupt state unless touched by the hand of the Master. In His hand its poverty can be transformed to plenitude, its helplessness to hope, its emptiness to joy and beauty.

The central fact of our most holy faith is that the God of our salvation *has* reached down from heaven and touched the hearts of men. In the words of the apostle Paul: "Ye know the grace of our Lord Jesus Christ, that though He was rich, yet for your sakes He became poor, that ye through His poverty might be rich." (2 Cor. 8:9)

Our lives, like the warped and broken-down piano in Albert Schweitzer's dining room, have "lost their poverty" in the Master's hands. Our lives have become rich and full — filled with the joy of our salvation.

And on our lips there has been placed a new song, the song of His redeemed: "Blessing and glory and wisdom and thanksgiving and honor and power and might be unto our God forever and ever." (Rev. 7:12)

Truly, we have lost our poverty — at the touch of the Master!

In the Hollow of His Hand

*T*he old sailor knew his Bible well. When asked if he was not afraid when the winds blew stiff and strong and his ship seemed at the mercy of the surging waves, he gave an answer each of us might well remember.

"No, I'm never completely afraid," he said. "The Good Book tells me that the Lord holds the waters in the hollow of His hands; so, even if my ship were wrecked and I'd fall into the sea, I'd only drop into my Father's hand."

What a graphic way of expressing the Christian doctrine of the omnipotence and loving providence of God! Or, still better, what a graphic way of describing the certainty of the believer's ultimate destiny! No matter what the adversity or calamity, when the calamity is over, he will still be in the hollow of his Father's hand.

Even if that calamity is — death!

Nor is this an assurance the believer has arrived at by some sort of "natural religion." It is an assurance that has been given him by Christ Himself.

To every believer Christ says: "My sheep hear My voice, and I know them, and they follow Me. And I give unto them eternal life, and they shall never perish, neither shall any man pluck them out of My hand. My Father, which gave them Me, is greater than all, and no man is able to pluck them out of My Father's hand. I and My Father are one." (John 10:27-30)

Are we sufficiently conscious of this glorious assurance from day to day? And do we appreciate it fully? By His vicarious suffering and death "for our offenses" and by His victorious resurrection "for our justification" Christ has, as it were, placed us into the hollow of His loving Father's hand — forever secure, reserved for His eternal kingdom.

Let tragedy or misfortune come, disappointment or disillusionment, yes, let *death* come and snatch us out of the land of the living — it can only drop us into the hollow of our Father's hand.

> We have Christ's word for that!
>
> Thine forever, Lord of Life!
> Shield us through our earthly strife.
> Thou, the Life, the Truth, the Way,
> Guide us to the realms of day.

Heavenly Arithmetic

*T*here is a legend about the lad who gave up his five barley loaves and two small fishes so that Christ could feed the hungry multitude. It tells how the boy hurried home, after all the fragments had been gathered, and told his mother all about the wonderful Man and the wonderful miracle.

With his eyes still big with excitement, he told her how his five little barley cakes and two dried fishes had multiplied in the Savior's hand until there was enough to feed five thousand famished people.

And then, with a wistful look, he added: "I wonder, Mother, whether it would be that way with *everything* you gave Him!"

It is only a legend, of course. Yet the haunting question of the lad deserves an answer. And the answer, as many can attest, is a frank and forthright: "Yes, my lad, in a sense it is that way with *everything* we give the Savior. He has a way of multiplying everything we hand Him and giving it back to us a hundredfold."

The omnipotent Son of God, who fed the multitudes on the hillsides of Galilee, is still the great Multiplier. Many a humble believer can testify to the unsearchable arithmetic whereby Christ has accepted a gift from one of His own and then has returned it — with added blessings beyond all expectation.

Many a pious mother who has been faithful in her stewardship, dedicating, as it were, her few loaves and fishes to the

Savior and His service, has suddenly become aware of His omnipotent, multiplying hand. "How did we ever do so much with so little?"

The apostle Paul assured the early Christians: "My God shall supply all your need according to His riches in glory by Christ Jesus" (Phil. 4:19). *His* God, the God who had revealed Himself through Jesus Christ, the Savior, was "able to do exceeding abundantly above all that we ask or think." (Eph. 3:20)

There is a sort of heavenly arithmetic whereby the humble gifts of God's children — the cup of water to the thirsty, the piece of bread to the hungry, the deed of loving service in His kingdom — come back with unexpected interest. Not always in the form of demonstrable, material blessings, to be sure, but in ways that are determined by Him who is able to do exceeding abundantly above all that we ask or think.

And so to the wistful boy from the Galilean hills we say: "Yes, my lad, in a sense it is that way with *everything* we give the Savior. He has a way of multiplying everything we hand Him and giving it back to us a hundredfold."

"In Me — Peace"

---

*T*wo artists vied with each other to see which could produce a painting that would best depict the idea of peace.

One painted the picture of a quiet lake away up on a mountaintop. Not a breeze was stirring. Not a bird was flying. Not a ripple disturbed the quiet waters. All was perfect silence. That, in the opinion of the first artist, was the truest picture of peace.

The second artist painted a picture of a roaring waterfall with a mighty oak overarching it. In the crotch of a limb bending low over the turbulent waters, almost within reach of the rising spray, he painted a tiny sparrow sitting calm and unperturbed in her little nest.

In the midst of the mighty roar, surrounded by what seemed to be frightful danger, the sparrow hadn't a worry in the world: her cozy little nest was snug in the crotch of a sturdy oak — on a branch which the waters could never reach.

Both artists agreed that the second picture came closer to depicting the highest conception of peace. Perhaps neither of them knew that in the second painting they had portrayed most beautifully that wonderful peace a Christian believer has found in his Savior.

The true peace and rest of the Christian life is not something to be found in a distant, idyllic never-never land; it is rather a peace and rest that is to be found right here and now — in the very midst of a world of trial and trouble.

Jesus told His disciples and us: *"Peace* I leave with you, *My* peace I give unto you; not as the world giveth give I unto you" (John 14:27). And again: "These things have I spoken unto you that in Me ye might have *peace.* In the world ye shall have tribulation; but be of good cheer; I have overcome the world." (John 16:33)

In the world — tribulation! In Christ — peace! This can be, because the Christ in whom we dwell has overcome the world in which we live. No matter how close the peril, how bitter the pain, how fierce the storm, we are at peace in Him who has overcome our darkest enemies: sin, death, hell, and Satan.

The prophet Isaiah has said it well: "Thou wilt keep him in perfect peace whose mind is stayed on Thee" (Is. 26:3). No matter what his circumstance in life, the believing Christian has "stayed his mind" on Jesus Christ, his omnipotent Redeemer.

The Ten Commandments — Ours to Keep

*O*ne day an old friend of Mark Twain told the humorist that it was his life's ambition to visit the Holy Land and to see the place where God had given the Ten Commandments to Moses.

Knowing that his friend's behavior over the years had left very much to be desired, Mark Twain sized him up for a moment, looked him straight in the eye, and said: "Why don't you just stay home and *keep* the Ten Commandments?"

We can read some practical theology into the humorist's reply.

It is so much easier to lecture on the Ten Commandments than to live them. So much easier to let our religion become an academic study than to let it be an active force in our daily lives. So much easier to view the whole Christian vocation as a course to be studied than as a course to be *run*.

Similarly, on a different level of our Christian life, it is so much easier to genuflect before an altar, make the sign of the cross, and repeat the words of an ancient liturgy than it is to *worship* our Lord in spirit and in truth. The real thing is always much more difficult.

Micah the prophet was painfully aware of this all too human tendency to substitute form for function, observance for obedience, and liturgy for life. He wrote: "Wherewith shall I come before the Lord and bow myself before the high God? Shall I come before Him with burnt offerings, with calves of a year old? Will the Lord be pleased with thousands of rams, or with ten thousands of rivers of oil? Shall I give my firstborn for my transgression, the fruit of my body for the sin of my soul? He hath showed thee, O man, what is good; and what doth the Lord require of thee but to do justly and to love mercy and to walk humbly with thy God?" (Micah 6:6-8)

Not the spectacular! But the humble walk with God from day to day — doing justly and loving mercy — that is what the Lord of heaven requires of us. Not standing on the spot where His commandments were given, but living in the Spirit who enables us to *keep* them more and more.

Thank God, we have a Savior who kept those commandments for us and who by His bitter suffering and death paid for our transgressions! Only by faith in *Him* shall we be able to walk closer and closer to that perfection which God expects of us.

Him We Can Trust

*D*wight L. Moody had spoken long and earnestly to the young man who had come to his study, seeking relief from a burden of guilt. In an effort to assure the young man of God's readiness to forgive, the kindly evangelist had repeated many of the Savior's precious promises.

Among the many passages he had quoted were the Savior's words of invitation and promise: "Come unto Me, all ye that labor and are heavy laden, and I will give you rest." (Matt. 11:28)

Disconsolate and unable to find comfort in any of the quoted passages, the young man exclaimed in desperation: "I just *can't believe!*" To which the evangelist was quick to reply: "*Whom* can't you believe?"

The young man sat silent for a moment. The words of the wise evangelist had struck home. Suddenly it dawned on the penitent young sinner that it was Christ whom he was refusing to believe. Christ — and not the kindly gentleman before him! And with that realization came the first stirring of a newfound faith.

It was Christ, not Dwight L. Moody, who had said: "Take My yoke upon you and learn of Me, for I am meek and lowly in heart; and ye shall find rest for your souls. For My yoke is easy, and My burden is light." (Matt. 11:29-30)

How important that we learn and relearn the lesson that young man took home with him that night! In the church as we know it today it is so easy for us (unconsciously perhaps) to base our hope of heaven on what the pastor says, or on what the catechism says, or on the latest pronouncement of our church body.

All of these, of course, are important and have their rightful place. But in the hour of trial, in the day of temptation, on a sickbed, or when the angel of death is hovering around our pillow we will want to know, above all else, what *Jesus* says. It is He and He alone who is worthy of our ultimate trust. For He and He alone is the omnipotent, omniscient, omnipresent "Word of God incarnate." He and no one else.

It is Christ, and no lesser authority, who tells us: "He that heareth My Word and believeth on Him that sent Me hath everlasting life and shall not come into condemnation but is passed from death to life" (John 5:24). It is the eternal Christ, and no mere man, who has given us the sublime assurance: "I am the Resurrection and the Life; he that believeth in Me, though he were dead, yet shall he live; and whosoever liveth and believeth in Me shall never die." (John 11:25)

Him we can trust. *Him* we can believe. On *Him* we can stake our soul for time and for eternity.

"Here Be God!"

We are told that many years ago, before the days of accurate maps, navigators drew up charts to describe what lay beyond the horizons of the distant seas.

On these were outlined vast unexplored waters over which the ancient geographers had written such weird legends as "Here be dragons," "Here be demons," or "Here be sirens."

One of these charts came to the attention of a master mariner who was also a devout believer. Irritated by what he read, he crossed out the superstitious legends and with bold strokes wrote in their place: "Here be God!"

Which reminds us of an incident recorded in the gospels. The disciples had spent a fearful night on the Sea of Galilee. Their little boat had been tossed to and fro by the churning waves.

Just before daybreak they saw a figure on the water, advancing toward them. Frozen with fear, they shouted their unanimous conviction: "It is a ghost!" In their terror they imagined they saw a vengeful spirit from the unseen world, bent on their destruction.

And while they still cringed in horror and dismay, they suddenly heard the reassuring voice of their familiar Friend coming across the surging water: "Be of good cheer; it is I; be not afraid!" (Matt. 14:27)

How prone we are (all of us) to follow the example either of the superstitious mariners of old or of the frightened disciples of our Lord! When life becomes difficult, when storm clouds begin to lower, when the waves of adversity begin to batter against our frail ship of life, we can see nothing but demons, dragons, ghosts — all combined in a hellish conspiracy to destroy us.

How quick we are to forget the blessed assurance of our Christian faith that in the midst of every storm that befalls the child of God there is not a dragon, not a demon, not a ghost — but a loving Lord! No matter how dark the night, how deep the wave, how strong the wind, the voice speaking to the Christian heart is still the same: "It is I; be not afraid."

In days of doubt or depression, sickness or sorrow, defeat or despair let us call upon our Lord for strength. Let us with bold strokes cross out the legend, "Here be demons." And with strokes of equal boldness let us write: "Here be God!"

"A Gloomy Moment in History"

*R*ecently we read a gloomy editorial dark with dire foreboding. Before we comment, we should like to quote just a few paragraphs.

"It is a gloomy moment in history," the editorial observed. "Not for many years, not in the lifetime of most men who read this paper, has there been so much grave and deep apprehension. Never has the future seemed so incalculable as at this time.

"In France the political caldron seethes and bubbles with uncertainty. Russia hangs as usual, like a cloud, dark and silent upon the horizon of Europe. All the energies, resources, and influences of the British Empire are sorely tried, and are yet to be tried more sorely. . . .

"It is a solemn moment. . . . Of our own troubles here in the United States no man can see the end."

When do you think the above editorial was written? Last week? last month? last year? No, these words first appeared, just as they are reproduced above, in *Harper's Weekly* under the dateline Oct. 10, 1857.

The editorial is more than a hundred years old, and yet, at least in its tone, it sounds no different from many an editorial that will appear in tomorrow morning's newspaper. "It is a gloomy moment in history. . . ." It would seem that history has had *many* gloomy moments!

We are reminded of a few verses in our Bible: "What has been is what will be, and what has been done is what will be done; and there is nothing new under the sun. Is there a thing of which it is said, 'See, this is new'? It has been already in the ages before us." (Eccl. 1:9-10 RSV)

This is not to minimize the many and distressing problems besetting the human family on every side today. The problems of our day are real, and their solution will call for the best, the highest, and the noblest that is in us.

It is rather to remind us that the God of history did not desert His world (the world which He *so loved,* John 3:16) on the morning after the *Harper's* editorial was written back in 1857. He continued to guide the destinies of men and nations — and to enfold in His arms of mercy all those who came to Him through faith in His beloved Son.

The God of history is the God who has revealed Himself to us in the face of Jesus Christ, our Savior and Lord. For us the present moment in history may indeed be shrouded in deepest gloom; but through Christ we know that He who is above, beneath, and behind the gloom is the very God who has made His face to shine upon us and who, in the hour of judgment, has promised to be gracious. Well might we heed the poet's words:

> Ye fearful saints, fresh courage take;
> The clouds ye so much dread
> Are big with mercy and shall break
> In blessing on your head.

"What's New?"

We have a friend who has an unusual but commendable habit. Frequently when asked by an associate or acquaintance, "What's new?" he replies quickly and simply, but with a knowing twinkle in his eye, "John three, sixteen."

To him there is much more in that reply than a superficial or perfunctory Christian witness. To him those three short words are the expression of the profoundest philosophy as well as the profoundest theology. As indeed they are!

Can there ever be anything newer, more startling, more demanding of our everyday attention than the eternal headline emblazoned in John three, sixteen?

And can there ever be *better* news than the timeless message: "God so loved the world that He gave His only-begotten Son that whosoever believeth in Him should not perish but have everlasting life"?

Many of last month's headlines have already faded into insignificance. Many of today's headlines will mean very little when we bundle our papers for next month's paper drive. There is something ephemeral, transitory, impermanent in almost every bit of this world's news. For a few moments it is new, then it is old, and soon it is forgotten, as it deserves to be.

Not so the news of John three, sixteen. Not only is it new for each succeeding generation, but it is also new each morning and each evening in the life of the believer.

There is not a moment in the life of any man when the

message of John three, sixteen is old, unsuited, or irrelevant. If it is true that we "daily sin much," it is also true that we daily need very much to hear the good news of the eternal headline of God's love and mercy in Jesus Christ, our Savior.

Much may happen in your life and mine before another sun will set. Some of it may be "new" — as we have learned to measure newness. But of this we can be sure: nothing will happen to us that will be more genuinely, more permanently, more eternally new than the ageless message God has given us in John three, sixteen.

He who has learned, as did the ancient prophet, that the Lord's mercies are new to him every morning has his own inner answer to the daily question, *What's new?*

In the Hands of God

*A*fter the battle lines of the Protestant Reformation were clearly drawn, the life of Martin Luther was in serious danger on more than one occasion.

We are told that when the heat of the conflict was at fever pitch, a dignitary of the church sought to frighten the great Reformer. He pointed to the overwhelming power, both ecclesiastical and political, that was arrayed against the lonely monk.

"Unless you can muster a force of equal strength in your defense," the churchman thundered, "where will you *be?*"

After a silent moment Martin Luther replied undaunted: "I shall be where I have always been — in the hands of Almighty God."

Do we have the same conviction as we go about our God-appointed tasks from day to day?

When we arise from bed each morning, when we set out for work, when we tackle the problems of another day, do we do so in the full consciousness that our lives are indeed "in the hands of Almighty God"?

When serious problems arise, when ominous clouds hang low on the horizon, when troubles mount, when fears annoy and doubts assail us, when sickness strikes, when death seems near, do we feel ourselves (as did Martin Luther) being safely held "in the hands of Almighty God"?

King David, a man after God's own heart, whose life was a constant succession of dangers and for whom disillusionment seemed to lurk at every corner, found confidence and courage in the knowledge that "my times are in *Thy hand*." (Ps. 31:15)

The Savior, speaking of those who would put their trust in Him, once said: "My sheep hear My voice, and I know them, and they follow Me, and I give unto them eternal life; and they shall never perish, neither shall any man pluck them out of *My hand*." (John 10:27-28)

As believers in Christ we need to cultivate the daily awareness that we are indeed in the hands of the Almighty. What a difference it would make if in every circumstance of life — in joy or sorrow, health or sickness, wealth or poverty, triumph or defeat — we could always see ourselves exactly where we are: in *His* hands!

The Grand Perspective

A group of boys was trying to see who could make the straightest track across a field of freshly fallen snow.

Again and again, to their dismay, they found that their feet had zigzagged from the path they had set out to follow. Determined to go straight, they had nevertheless gone crooked.

Finally the youngest among them surprised them all. He succeeded in making a path that was almost as straight as a rule, deviating neither to the right nor to the left.

When asked how he managed to do it, he said: "It was easy. I just kept my eyes on that lightning rod on top of the barn over there, while the rest of you were always looking at your feet."

Perhaps there is a lesson for life in those sage words of the youngster. How many of us stumble through day after day, looking only at our feet! Looking only at the task at hand! Only at the moment that lies immediately before us!

It is true, the task at hand may be important, and the challenge of the present moment may demand our best. But like the youngster who gave his best to every step by keeping his eyes fixed on the rod above the barn, so we, too, shall be able to give our best to every moment only if every moment is part of a grand perspective.

The Bible puts it this way. "Let us run with patience the race that is set before us, *looking unto Jesus,* the Author and Finisher of our faith, who for the joy that was set before Him endured the cross, despising the shame, and is set down at the right hand of the throne of God." (Heb. 12:1-2)

Looking unto Jesus! That is the ultimate focus of the grand perspective. In the measure in which we learn to fix our eyes on Him, in that measure we shall find our lives "going straight and in the right direction."

The Savior once said: "And I, if I be lifted up from the earth, will draw all men unto Me" (John 12:32). Like a mighty magnet, He draws us to Himself not only that we might be His own but also that we might walk in the paths which He has chosen.

Once we have fixed our eyes of faith firmly on Him who stands at the open door of our Father's house, always beckoning, always drawing, we shall find every step along the way falling into the grand perspective.

> Draw us to Thee;
> Oh, grant that we
> May walk the road to heaven!
> Direct our way
> Lest we should stray
> And from Thy paths be driven.

Will Tomorrow Be Different?

*I*t was New Year's Eve. The winter sky was clear and the evening air crisp as little Tommy and his parents walked hand in hand toward the lighted church at the far end of the street.

After several moments of thoughtful silence the boy looked up at his mother and earnestly inquired: "Mommy, will tomorrow *really* be different?"

Not sure what was in the youngster's mind, his mother replied: "Why— what do you mean?"

"When Daddy was reading at the supper table tonight," Tommy explained, "he said that tomorrow God would give us a brand new year. . . . Will He?"

"Yes, dear. It will be a brand new year," she assured the inquiring 5-year-old.

Tommy thought a while and then, with the brilliant insight reserved only for candidates for kindergarten, he inquired eagerly: "Well, if it's new, will it be different?"

Perhaps each of us would do well to ponder Tommy's question on our way to church this New Year's Eve. Will the brand new year that lies ahead be any different from the old? Or will it be merely a carbon copy, a repeat, a rerun of the year now coming to an end?

Our heavenly Father does not expect the new year to be the same as the old. Not for those who will spend the new year in the spiritual fellowship of His Son! For them He expects the coming year to be not only *new* but also *different*.

He expects next year to be different for you and me, because we are to "grow in grace and in the knowledge of our Lord and Savior Jesus Christ" (2 Peter 3:18). We are to "grow up into Him . . . which is the Head, even Christ." (Eph. 4:15)

For those who are growing up in Christ the future can never be exactly the same as the past. Each day, each year is different. Each day, each year is richer in the personal experience of His grace. For with every passing scene of life the believer is *growing up* into the stature of Jesus Christ, His Savior.

We are not doing violence to the words of Paul if we paraphrase them to read: "Therefore, if any man be in Christ, he is constantly becoming a new creature; old things are constantly passing away; behold, all things are constantly becoming new." (2 Cor. 5:17)

And so, to little Tommy's question we would answer: Yes, Tommy, the brand new year which God will give us tomorrow will be different.

It will be different because you and I and all who believe in Jesus are going to do everything we possibly can, with God's help, to *make* it different.

Which One?

*T*he pastor was speaking to a hardened sinner who was outspoken in his disdain for the church.

"When I'm good and ready, I'll still have time to think about religion," was the man's reply to the pastor's pleading.

"But how do you know the Lord will give you an opportunity to repent and to believe — before death ushers you into eternity? Do you think it wise or safe to postpone setting your spiritual house in order until the eleventh hour?"

With a smirk of satisfaction on his wizened face the hardened sinner replied: "Remember the thief on the cross?"

The sage old pastor fixed his gaze steadily on the man in front of him and replied quietly: "Which one?"

Yes — which one? For one of the malefactors on the cross the eleventh hour had proved the vestibule of hell. It had not proved the open door to heaven. For him there was no moment of repentance, no moment of faith.

He died as he had lived, and on the other side of death he would have to live as he had died — forever separated, forever alienated from the God of his salvation.

It is true that in God's gracious providence there is always the possibility of an eleventh-hour conversion. One of the malefactors did repent in his final hour and was privileged to hear the words of the Savior: "Today thou shalt be with Me in Paradise." (Luke 23:43)

But we must always remember that there were *two* malefactors in the Passion story. And for one of them the eleventh hour proved too late. It is both foolhardy and dangerous to postpone the moment of repentance and faith — even for a single hour.

The apostle Paul tells us: "Behold, *now* is the accepted time; behold, *now* is the day of salvation" (2 Cor. 6:2). Thank God that for each of us *today* is the day of grace.

Today we have our Lord's assurance that "though your sins be as scarlet, they shall be as white as snow; though they be red like crimson, they shall be as wool" (Is. 1:18). And how can this be? Because "the blood of Jesus Christ, His Son, cleanseth us from all sin." (1 John 1:7)

That invitation, that offer, that assurance is ours today.

Today Thy mercy calls us
    To wash away our sin.
However great our trespass,
    Whatever we have been,
However long from mercy
    Our hearts have turned away,
Thy precious blood can cleanse us
    And make us white today.

You and I will do well to heed the date on the Gospel invitation God has addressed to you and me. It is dated *today!*

Valleys of Refreshment

*T*he Bible abounds in passages that have both a prosaic and a poetic meaning. Sometimes we arrive at the deepest and broadest meaning of these passages only after a fusing of both the prosaic and the poetic.

The familiar fourth verse of Psalm 23, for instance, really reads: "Even though I walk through the valley of great darkness." Poetically (and the Psalms *are* poetry) the psalmist was speaking of course of "the valley of the shadow of death."

There is a similar passage in Psalm 84 that reads: "As they go through the valley of Baca, they make it a place of springs" (v. 6 RSV). The word "Baca" here refers to the balsam trees that grew in certain valleys of Palestine and shed, as it were, great *tears* of gum. So in the poet's mind Baca conjured up the picture of weeping.

Some have therefore translated this verse: "As they go through the valley of weeping, they make it a place of springs." The psalmist is referring to the Jews who lived in distant places and to the many hardships they had to endure in their long and sometimes perilous pilgrimages to the temple at Jerusalem.

"As they go through the valley of weeping, they make it a place of springs." What a picture of your earthly pilgrimage and mine!

In our journey to the heavenly Jerusalem we must indeed traverse many a valley of weeping — the arduous toil of many a discouraging day; the fears, the frustrations that go with personal failure; the weariness of protracted illness; the piercing pain of personal bereavement; the piling up in our heart of hearts of a thousand unanswered "whys?"

Valleys of weeping indeed! But by God's grace we can make them "places of springs" — places of spiritual refreshment. We can do so by fixing our eyes, as it were, on the glittering dome of the majestic Jerusalem that lies ahead.

With our ultimate destination constantly before us, every valley becomes but another episode in our journey to the land which knows no tears (Rev. 7:17). Episodes are short. The final fruition of our Savior's promises in the heavenly Jerusalem will endure forever.

Let us follow His example, then, who "for the joy that was set before Him endured the cross, despising the shame." (Heb. 12:2)

With our eyes fixed firmly on the joy that has been set before us, you and I can find refreshment in the valley — even in the valley of tears.

A Famine of God's Word

*R*ecently a devout believer who lives in one of the Baltic countries behind the Iron Curtain wrote to a relative in Chicago. "Nowhere can a Bible be purchased in our country," he said, "and we are surrounded by antireligious propaganda. If we want to mention the name of God, we must do so secretly."

And he ended his pathetic letter with the following touching words: "We do not starve for bread and water, but we hunger to hear the Word of the living God. Please ask our Christian brethren there to pray for us."

What an indictment of our spiritually surfeited North America! We have Bibles without number, but millions never open them. We have churches on almost every corner, but millions never enter them. We hear the name of God on the street, in the factory, and in the office — but more often in profanity and blasphemy than in reverent Christian witness.

In the midst of our spiritual plenty we may well hang our heads in shame as we reread the closing words of our fellow believer behind the iron curtain: "We do not starve for bread and water, but we hunger to hear the Word of the living God."

In our affluence and freedom with its rich supply of the living Word, we may well heed the prophecy of the prophet Amos: "Behold, the days come, saith the Lord God, that I will send a famine in the land, not a famine of bread nor a thirst for water, but of hearing the words of the Lord. . . . They shall run to and fro to seek the Word of the Lord . . . and shall not find it." (Amos 8:11-12)

May this dire prophecy never find its fulfillment in our beloved land. To this end may we open our Bibles. May we "read, mark, learn, and inwardly digest" the life-giving message inscribed on its pages. May we crowd our churches so that we may be strengthened by the nourishing Word heralded from their pulpits. And may His precious Word be on our lips more frequently in faithful daily witness.

In order that we might be spared a famine of God's Word, may our prayer be that of the 17th-century poet:

> Lord Jesus Christ, with us abide,
> For round us falls the eventide;
> Nor let Thy Word, that heavenly light,
> For us be ever veiled in night.

The Shout of Easter

A Christian young man had prevailed upon an unbelieving friend to accompany him to church on Easter morning.
The minister read the account of the Savior's resurrection in
the Gospel for the day and then preached on the triumphant
words of Paul in the 15th chapter of First Corinthians: "O
death, where is thy sting? O grave, where is thy victory? The
sting of death is sin, and the strength of sin is the law. But
thanks be to God, which giveth us the *victory* through our
Lord Jesus Christ."

In glowing terms he spoke of the glories of the Christian
life, dwelling impressively on its victory over sin, death, and
the power of the grave. With eloquent fervor he proclaimed
the Christian's certainty of final resurrection and eternal life
with Jesus Christ, his Savior.

With a jubilant conviction that swept over the entire
congregation the minister quoted the well-known hymn: "He
lives and grants me daily breath; He lives, and I shall conquer
death; He lives my mansion to prepare; He lives to bring me
safely there."

On the way home from church the Christian young man
asked his friend what he thought of the service. He replied:
"If I believed what your minister said, I'd spend the rest of my
life shouting about it. I don't see how anyone could believe
what he said and then just go home as if he hadn't heard it."

What an indictment — and what a challenge!

We who have heard the Easter message year after year,

102

have we learned to shout about it? Have we learned not only to "come and see" but also to "go and tell"? Have we learned to spread the incredible news that He is risen?

Surely this is news too good to keep! The Son of God who was dead is gloriously *alive.* And we have His pledge and promise that because *He* lives, *we,* too, shall live. Could the God of heaven have given us any headline more thrilling, more electrifying, more worthy of being shouted from the housetops — not only on Easter morning but on every morning of the year?

As we leave our houses of worship on Easter Sunday — on *every* Sunday — may our hearts be bursting with the ineffable joy of our Savior's resurrection. And may that joy find eloquent expression in our daily lives. Then we shall experience the holy rapture of the poet who exclaimed:

> Oh, that I had a thousand voices
> To praise my God with thousand tongues!
> My heart, which in the Lord rejoices,
> Would then proclaim in grateful songs
> To all, wherever I might be,
> What great things God hath done for me.

He Put the World Together

*I*t was one of the first long evenings of autumn, and 5-year-old Andy was finding time heavy on his hands.

In an effort to keep the youngster occupied his father got out a well-worn jigsaw puzzle, spread it on the living room floor, and suggested that Andy try to put it together.

"When you've put all the pieces together, you'll have the whole world with all the continents and all the oceans," he said.

It was only a few minutes later when the youngster surprised his father by tugging at his shirtsleeve and asking: "*Now* what should I do, Daddy?"

"Do you mean you've put the whole world together already?" "Aw, it was easy. I knew there was a man on the other side of it. So I just put the man together, and *that* put the world together."

Little Andy of course didn't know it, but he had just given voice to a profound theological truth which the church of our day well might ponder. "I just put the man together, and *that* put the world together."

What our broken world needs today more than new treaties, new alliances, new missiles, new master plans is new *men* — men who have been transformed by the redeeming, converting, and sanctifying power of God. It is broken *man* who needs to be "put together" first if a new day is to dawn for our broken world.

Reginald Heber, in a different age and under different circumstances, expressed the same thought when he wrote in his well-known mission hymn:

> What though the spicy breezes
> Blow soft o'er Ceylon's isle;
> Though every prospect pleases,
> And only *man* is vile. . . .

All the powers of the material universe, all the wisdom of the wise, all the strategy of the most brilliant minds will not succeed in putting the world (that is, the human family) together until *man himself* has been "put together" by a power and wisdom much higher than himself.

The church of Jesus Christ has that power. It has that power in the Gospel of redemption which it has been commissioned to preach. The Scriptures tell us: "If any man be in Christ, he is a new creature; old things are passed away; behold, all things are become new." (2 Cor. 5:17)

The Gospel of Christ takes old men and makes new men of them. New women. New children. New creations. All "little Christs," as Martin Luther calls them. All eager to serve their Lord and their fellowman. All dedicated to seek the welfare of the broken, bleeding world in which they live.

Well might we all remember the unconscious wisdom of little Andy who said: "I just put the *man* together, and that put the *world* together."

Allergic to Yourself?

A conscientious Christian had paid several visits to a competent psychiatrist. In a moment of utter frankness she finally confronted him with the blunt question: "Doctor, what *is* wrong with me?"

Taken aback momentarily, he stroked his jaw as he searched for the proper answer. "Well," he said, "if you want my tentative diagnosis, I'd say you're allergic to yourself. If there's one person you ought to stay away from, it's *you*."

Without going into the technical aspects involved, there *is* an "allergy to oneself" against which the sensitive Christian must be on his guard, perhaps even more so than his unbelieving friends and neighbors.

We find a classical case record of this type of self allergy in the seventh chapter of Paul's Letter to the Romans. The more Paul looked inward into his inmost, deepest self, the more he saw a titanic struggle going on.

He saw two forces locked in mortal combat. There was the *old* nature that he had inherited by virtue of his natural birth, and there was the *new* nature that had been given him as a result of his rebirth in Jesus Christ, his Savior. These two natures, the apostle laments, were in a constant state of civil war within him.

As a result he complained most bitterly: "I find myself doing the very evil things which I know are wrong and which I detest, and at the same time I find myself failing to do all those good things upon which I've resolved most nobly."

So acute was this constant warfare within the heart of the great apostle that he finally exclaimed: "Miserable creature that I am, who is there to rescue me out of this body doomed to death? God alone, through Jesus Christ our Lord! Thanks be to God! (Rom. 7:24-25 NEB)

There is only one who can rescue us from the brutal struggle going on within us between our two opposing natures. "God alone, through Jesus Christ our Lord!" He has not guaranteed an immediate cessation of hostilities, but He has placed upon our hearts the seal of final victory.

Through Christ He has assured us of full and free forgiveness of all the evil machinations of our old, rebellious, sinful self. We shall never be free from sin in this mortal life, but we shall be free from its guilt, its dominion, and its punishment. This is the message of the cross.

And through Christ the God of heaven has also promised to empower and enable us so that we might cope ever more successfully with the wily foe within us. (Phil. 4:13)

Allergic to yourself? Take Christ with you into each new day. He'll tilt the balance of the battle in your favor.

When God Moves In

*T*he story is told of an artist who walked two miles to his studio each morning. Halfway to the studio he would slow his pace each day to admire an old ramshackle dwelling that had stood vacant for many years.

To the view of the ordinary passerby the house was nothing but an eyesore — with its tumbledown porch, its loose-hanging shutters, and its broken windows. But to the imaginative eye of the artist there was something fascinating about the gracefully sprawling structure.

Finally, in response to an irresistible urge, he bought the house and moved into it. Once it was his, he began to make the improvements of which he had dreamed over many months.

Week by week and month by month the old mansion took on a new appearance as it reflected the touch of its new master, until finally in place of the ugly and disreputable old building that had marred the neighborhood for years there stood a gleaming-white dwelling of striking grace and beauty. A center of attraction for the entire community!

And all because an artist had bought it, had moved into it, and had taken over.

That is exactly what God has done for you and me. Through Christ He has bought us, and through the working of His Holy Spirit He has moved into our lives and taken over. It was the blaspheming Saul, turned Christian Paul, who said: "Christ liveth in me. And the life which I now live . . . I live by the faith of the Son of God, who loved me and gave Himself for me." (Gal. 2:20)

Paul's life had been anything but attractive or beautiful until Christ Himself stepped in and reshaped his life to suit Christ's purposes. From the moment Christ "took hold of him," Paul's life underwent a progressive transformation. His one desire was to become more and more like the One who owned him. (Phil. 3:12-14)

In an eloquent passage in First Corinthians Paul reminds the early Christians: "Know ye not that your body is the temple of the Holy Ghost, which is in you, which ye have of God, and ye are not your own? For ye are bought with a price; therefore glorify God in your body and in your spirit, which are God's." (1 Cor. 6:19-20)

Indeed, you and I are not only the purchase of God's love; we are His earthly dwelling place. "He in us." The question you and I might well ask ourselves each day is: Does our life reflect the beauty and the glory of Him who has purchased us and who dwells in us?

Go, Tell It on the Mountain!

*I*t happened shortly after the successful launching of Telstar, the spectacular communications satellite. A learned space scientist had been addressing a group of his peers and was bringing his lecture to a close.

After having eloquently described the world as a ready-made audience sitting, as it were, in our own back yard, eager to see and hear whatever we may project, he paused a moment and then quietly asked the rhetorical question: "Gentlemen, what are we going to *tell* it?"

What are we going to tell a waiting world?

The irony of our age is that we have developed the science of communication to a degree of which our fathers would never have dared to dream; but all of a sudden the realization has dawned on us that we are not sure we have anything worthwhile to communicate.

How eagerly the prophets of old would have seized upon the opportunities of a Telstar! Listen to the fervor of an Isaiah: "O Zion [O Church], that bringest good tidings, get thee up into the high mountain! O Jerusalem [O Church], that bringest good tidings, lift up thy voice with strength; lift it up, be not afraid; say unto the cities of Judah, Behold your God!" (Is. 40:9)

What the Eleven would have done if they had had access to a Telstar on the day their resurrected Lord gave them their great commission: "Go ye, therefore, and teach all nations"! (Matt. 28:19)

After they had seen their victorious Lord ascend visibly into the heavens, what they would have done with a Telstar as they recalled His parting words: "Ye shall be witnesses unto Me . . . unto the uttermost part of the earth"! (Acts 1:8)

Is there any doubt what these men would have done if they had had access to communications media such as we have today? Surely they would have made the welkin ring with the electrifying message: "Hear, O world! The God of all creation has sent His Son into our very midst. He has lived with us — died for us — risen again — and returned into the heavens. Of these things we are witnesses. Salvation is only in His name."

The church of the 20th century has essentially the same message as did the faithful few who returned to Jerusalem from Mount Olivet on the day of the ascension. Will we be as faithful as they — in getting out the message to a world which, almost literally, is being gathered "in our own backyard"?

> Salvation! Oh, Salvation!
> The joyful sound proclaim
> Till earth's remotest nation
> Has learned Messiah's name.

"Just As If . . ."

A week had passed since the Sunday school teacher had done her best to explain to her children the meaning of the Bible word "justified."

In her own opinion she had failed quite miserably.

And so on this particular Sunday she thought she would determine the extent of her success or failure. Among her review questions she asked:

"What does the Bible mean when it says that we've been 'justified' by God?"

There was a moment of silence. Then a lad, whose deportment had caused the teacher many a trying moment in the past, raised his hand and began to speak slowly and thoughtfully.

"When the Bible says I'm justified," he said, "it means, no matter what I've done bad, God is willing to look at me *just-if-I'd* never done it."

We may not be ready to give this lad an A in English, but on the basis of his answer he certainly deserved an A in religion. In his own way he had given voice to exactly what the Bible means when it says that you and I have been justified.

The central message of the Scriptures, as a matter of fact, is precisely this: No matter what you and I have done, no matter how many or how great our transgressions, God is willing to look upon us *just as if* we had never done them. He is willing to do this because of what Jesus Christ, our Lord and Savior, has done for us.

St. Paul puts this Bible doctrine very clearly in his letter to the Romans. He says that we have been "justified *freely* (that is, without the payment of any price on our part) by His *gra*ce (that is, by God's undeserved love and mercy) through the *redemption* that is in Christ Jesus (that is, through His great act of atonement on our behalf), whom God hath set forth to be a *propitiation* (that is, a payment) through faith in His *blood* (that is, His death on the cross)." (Rom. 3:24-25)

To the Philippians Paul boasted that he had no righteousness of his own. The only righteousness to which he could lay claim was that which was his by faith in Jesus Christ. (Phil. 3:9)

Because of the perfect life, sinless death, and triumphant resurrection of Christ, his Savior (all on *his* behalf), Paul knew that his slate had been washed clean in the sight of his heavenly Father. His debt had been cancelled.

Indeed, God was looking at him "just as if" he had never sinned. And that is the way God is looking at you and me today.

With Paul you and I can say and exult: "There is therefore now no condemnation to them which are in Christ Jesus" (Rom. 8:1). No condemnation for you and me, because God is looking upon us *"just as if. . . ."*

We Can Trust Him All the Way!

*A*n elderly farmer had vowed that he would never ride in an airplane. Air travel is "for the birds" was his whimsical philosophy.

One day an emergency arose, and he found it necessary to take a plane to a distant city. When he arrived, eager relatives plied him with endless questions. How did he enjoy his first experience in the air?

"Oh, it was all right," he reckoned. "But I'll tell you *one* thing!" he continued in obstinate self-justification. "I never let my full weight down on that there seat."

Fearful lest the mighty jet was not powerful enough to carry his entire weight to his intended destination, he had sat in a tensed position, trying to share *his* portion of the burden!

We may smile at the humor of the picture, and yet isn't that a picture of some of us — in our journey through life? Sitting in a tensed position, insisting on carrying our share of the burden lest the good Lord find it impossible to bring us safely to our journey's end?

We know that He has invited us to cast *all* our cares on Him (1 Peter 5:7), but in our human foolishness we insist on clinging to some of our cares and struggling with them ourselves. Illness, financial difficulties, an uncertain future, approaching old age — one or two of these burdens we insist on carrying by ourselves, as if the good Lord weren't quite able to fulfill His promise of carrying "all" for us.

We know that underneath are the everlasting arms

(Deut. 33:27), but somehow we doubt that those arms are fully adequate to the task. We must add our strength to theirs! And so, like the old man on the plane, we never quite let our full weight down. We are never quite sure that the omnipotent arms of our God will bring us safely through.

Let us be done with sharing our burdens with the Almighty, as if they were to be carried 90 percent by Him and 10 percent by us. Let us place them wholly in His arms. He has promised to carry not only us but our burdens, too.

We who have learned to know a loving God through Jesus Christ, our Lord, can pray at the dawn of each new day:

> I am trusting Thee, Lord Jesus;
> Never let me fall.
> I am trusting Thee forever
> And for all.

115

The Stewardship of Old Age

A young pastor, newly graduated from a seminary, had just paid a house call to an elderly Christian couple. Both had been confined to their home for several years, due to the infirmities of old age.

The young man had spoken comfortingly to them, quoting a number of passages from Scripture, including the reassuring words of the Lord: "I will never leave thee nor forsake thee." (Heb. 13:5)

After he had gone, the elderly woman commented to her husband: "What a fine young man." Her husband leaned back in his chair, mused a moment, and then replied: "Yes, but he's goin' to have to do a heap of livin' before he knows what he just told us."

We don't have to agree fully with the old man of the house in order to get his point. To him the passing years had filled the comforting words of Scripture with a content that was still beyond the ability of the younger man to fathom. Years of sickness, pain, and suffering, years of fighting off the pursuing specter of pinching poverty had taught the old man the meaning of "I will never leave thee nor forsake thee" in a way that was still beyond the young man's grasp.

And so, quite understandably, he mused: "He's goin' to have to do a heap of livin' before he knows what he just told us."

It is no disparagement of youth to say that there is no substitute for spiritual experience, spiritual growth, and spiritual maturity. It was only after Job had successfully endured his indescribable anxiety of heart and mind and spirit that he could finally say: "I have heard of Thee by the hearing of the ear, *but now mine eye seeth Thee*" (Job 42:5). It had indeed taken a heap of living — and almost dying — to bring him to that insight.

It is a fact of Christian life that those who are older, those who have weathered the storms of life and on whose hands are the scars of many battles are frequently in the best position to share with others what their "eyes have seen." (Luke 2:30)

Perhaps this is the special stewardship of those who are veterans in the faith — to reach back to those who are still coming up and to strengthen their hands for the battle. To display their scars and bruises as the incontestable credentials of faithful servants of the King. To share with those behind them the vision of final victory which frequently is seen best by dimming eyes.

That the ministry of healing comfort is a special grace of those who have known the cares and crosses of life is eloquently told in the words of the unknown poet:

> He cannot heal who has not suffered much,
> For only sorrow, sorrow understands.
> They will not come for healing at our touch
> Who have not seen the scars upon our hands.

A General Christmas?

---

*T*he faithful and efficient secretary had set the afternoon aside for addressing Christmas cards for her boss.

On her desk before her were two stacks of cards — expensive and reflecting the good taste of her employer.

After addressing a dozen or more greetings, she approached her boss with the inquiry: "Which type of card should I send to Mr. Ross?"

After a long moment of reflection the man behind the large desk replied: "I'm not sure. He's a new client, and I don't know too much about him. Better send him the 'general Christmas.'"

And so, instead of receiving the card with the warm inscription "May the Christ of Christmas Bless You," Mr. Ross received the card with the richly embossed but Christless message, "Holiday Greetings."

How tragic that many a Christian today is willing to settle for a *general Christmas* not only for himself but also and especially for his friends, his neighbors, and his business associates.

For himself, while joining the faithful in their accustomed hours of worship, he is willing to confine his personal and family observance of the holy season to what the world would call a "merry Christmas."

In his dreams he goes back *not* to the "Gloria in Excelsis" as sung by the angelic chorus in the skies over Bethlehem, but merely to "A White Christmas" as sung by Bing Crosby in a

Hollywood recording studio. All his protestations to the contrary notwithstanding, his is in the main a general Christmas, a season of "holiday greetings."

As for Mr. Ross in the incident described above, no matter who he was, he needed nothing more than the intercessory prayer of his friend at Christmas: "May the Christ of Christmas Bless You."

The proclamation of the angel to the shepherds of Bethlehem was all inclusive: "Behold, I bring you good tidings of great joy, which shall be to *all people*" (Luke 2:10). All people, including Mr. Ross! The message of Christmas is in large part a missionary proclamation. All people are to hear the good news. The glad tidings "unto you is born a Savior" was meant for them. You and I have no right to withhold it.

Pray God that when the Feast of the Nativity comes this year, ours will not be a "general Christmas" — a season of mere "holiday greetings," no matter how warmly, how beautifully, or how expensively expressed.

May our hearts rather be filled with the wondrous story of the Babe of Bethlehem. And may our lips and our lives express our heartfelt prayer for those both near and far: "May the Christ of Christmas Bless You."

"One by One We Shall Conquer"

*I*t was during one of the many wars of ancient Greece. A small army was in hopeless retreat. Greatly outnumbered and unable to hold back the pursuing foe, the disorganized band of only a few hundred managed to make its way through a narrow mountain pass.

Once on the other side of the pass, their commander shouted a new command. "Stand! From *here* we can deal with the enemy." He explained: "No matter how many men they have, they must come to us through the narrow funnel of that pass. They must come to us one by one — and one by one we shall conquer."

The Captain of our salvation tells us something very similar each New Year's Eve as we stand at the narrow pass that divides the old year from the new. Beyond the pass, in the year still hidden from our view, lie problems and perplexities.

Our hearts quail at the prospect of another year of burdensome tasks, heavy responsibilities, and grave decisions. In our human frailty we are overwhelmed by the ominous possibilities of the unknown year that lies beyond our view.

But, thank God, each of those moments is in the hand of our gracious God, and He is going to let them come to us only one by one. And with each moment will come the needed grace and power. He has promised that as our days, so shall our strength be. (Deut. 33:25)

We have His assurance that each moment of the coming year will find us equipped with the amount of strength that will be necessary to bear its burden, to endure its trial, and to fight its battle through.

And so as we stand at the pass of each new year, let us not be frightened by the overwhelming greatness of its possibilities, but let us rather find comfort and strength in the knowledge that in God's good providence all the moments of the new year will be coming single file — one moment at a time. And for each moment His needed grace will be supplied. (Phil. 4:19)

> God does not lead me year by year
> Nor even day by day;
> But step by step my path unfolds
> As He directs my way.
> Tomorrow's plans I do not know:
> I only know this hour
> And Him who bids me walk each step
> Supported by His power.
> And I am glad that it is so:
> Today's enough to bear.
> And when tomorrow comes, His grace
> Will far exceed my care.
> What need to worry then or fret?
> My Lord, who gave His Son,
> Holds all my moments in His hand
> And gives them one by one.

Let us, then, not try to live tomorrow today. Let us not try to live February in January. Above all, let us not fear the prospect of the unknown future. God, the All-Wise, the Almighty, the Eternal — with whom there are no yesterdays and with whom there are no tomorrows — has gone ahead, and when we reach our own tomorrow, we will find Him there.

It's a Gift

A promising young student had spent almost an hour in the study of Helmuth Thielicke, the noted German theologian. At the conclusion of their discussion the young man rose politely and began to take leave of the respected professor.

As both men reached the study door, Dr. Thielicke observed: "You are a gifted young man." Embarrassed by the unexpected compliment, the young man *blushed* — with what we might term becoming modesty.

Noticing the young man's momentary embarrassment, the professor was quick to add: "Remember, I did not say you are a *brilliant* young man. I said you are *gifted*. God has given you remarkable talents. You will be responsible to Him for the way you use them."

How needful that reminder for every one of us! In moments when we are tempted to parade our superior accomplishments, when we are tempted to preen ourselves or to strut proudly before our fellowmen, let us remember that we have nothing that was not *given* us. All our abilities are gifts from our heavenly Father.

St. Paul chided his Corinthian Christians with the gentle rebuke: "What have you that you did not receive? If then you received it, why do you boast as if it were not a gift?" (1 Cor. 4:7 RSV). He was speaking particularly of the spiritual endowments that had become theirs through faith in Christ.

But he was not excluding their other endowments, all of which were gifts of the same heavenly Father: endowments of body, mind, and total personality. In chapter 12 of the same epistle he catalogs the "diversities of gifts" God has distributed to all believers.

To St. Paul there was no such thing as a brilliant preacher. He knew only *gifted* preachers, *gifted* teachers, *gifted* musicians, *gifted* artists, *gifted* housewives, *gifted* craftsmen — no matter what the craft may have been. He saw all worthwhile talents as coming from God.

And with every gift there comes a responsibility. Our Savior tells us: "Freely ye have received, freely give" (Matt. 10:8). We are to use our talents in the service of the Lord who gave them. They are still His talents. You and I have been gifted — so that by our gifts we may serve "the least of these His brethren."

> Lord, Thou hast brought to me
>   Down from Thy home above
> Salvation full and free,
>   Thy pardon and Thy love.
> Great gifts Thou broughtest me;
>   What have I brought to Thee?

"Unto a Land That *I* Will Show Thee"

We were dining with a friend in a rooftop restaurant overlooking the sprawling city of Los Angeles. It was night, and the shimmering lights of the city stretched out like lacy strings of beads sparkling against a background of soft and velvety black.

For more than an hour we sat there and discussed the incredible changes that had taken place in the world during the past few years. The tenor of our conversation was frankly nostalgic and mildly pessimistic.

Looking out over the teeming city, our friend observed almost sadly: "As long as you and I live there will never again be a routine day, a routine week, a routine month, a routine year."

How true! The routine days and weeks of yesteryear are gone forever. Ours is not only a time of rapid and cataclysmic change — it is also a time of violent and irreversible revolution. Our todays can scarcely recognize our yesterdays, and our tomorrows will be hard put to recognize today. And this is true in almost every area of life: in science and technology, in politics and government, in morals and religion.

The snug comfort of the world of our fathers, when yesterdays, todays, and tomorrows could be laid together end to end in a fairly predictable continuum, is rapidly becoming a faded memory. Whether we like to admit it or not, the snug, secure little world of our fathers is gone. It is *no more!*

The individual believer today is in very much the same position as was Abraham some four thousand years ago. To Abraham the Lord said: "Get thee out of thy country and from thy kindred and from thy father's house unto a land that I will show thee." (Gen. 12:1)

Abraham was to leave every symbol of security — his country, his kindred, his father's house — and travel to a land he had never seen. The only pledge of security he had for the journey into the uncharted future that lay before him was the promise of His Lord to be with him and to bless him.

You and I have that selfsame promise. He who has placed our feet upon an unknown path is leading us to a land that "*He* will show us." And we have the unbreakable promise of His Son that He will go with us all the way. "Lo, I am with you alway, even unto the end of the world." (Matt. 28:20)

Our tomorrows may be completely different from today. But when tomorrow comes, we may be sure there will be Someone at our side who never changes — "Jesus Christ, the same yesterday and today and forever." (Heb. 13:8)

We have no promise of a routine future. We *do* have the promise of an unchanging and unchangeable Christ. With Him at our side we can leave all yesterdays behind and walk securely into tomorrow — no matter *what* tomorrow holds.

"Not for a Million Dollars!"

A wealthy woman who had contributed large sums of money to Christian missions decided to make a trip around the world — to visit some of the mission stations that had been the beneficiaries of her generosity.

In country after country she was impressed by the modern facilities her financial offerings had helped make possible. She was eminently satisfied that the mission boards had invested her sizable benefactions wisely.

Finally she came to a faraway leper colony. In a small room in the dispensary she saw a young Christian nurse treating a putrid, festering sore on the body of an aged leper.

Revolted by what she saw, she exclaimed in horror: "I couldn't do that for a million dollars!"

"Neither could I," replied the young nurse quietly and simply as she looked up from her neat bandages into the shocked face of her wealthy visitor.

All the money in the world could not have persuaded her to work day after day amid the offensive odors and nauseating surroundings — far from the comforts of home and the companionship of loved ones.

And yet she was *here!* She was doing the very thing that all the money in the world could never have persuaded her to do. Why? Because a power far more persuasive, far more overwhelming than all the clanking cash in a thousand treasure chests had gotten hold of her heart and was now in complete control of her behavior.

That power was the love of Christ, the love that had redeemed her, body and soul, for time and eternity. As the apostle Paul put it: "The love of Christ *constraineth* (that is, controls and drives) us. . . . He died for all, that they which live should not henceforth live unto themselves but unto Him which died for them and rose again." (2 Cor. 5:14-15)

What a lesson in truly Christian motivation! Not for a million dollars — but for a Savior who died for all, "that they which live should not henceforth live unto themselves but unto *Him* which died for them and rose again."

The wealthy woman learned something that day — about the love of Christ and what miracles it can perform in the human heart. In the humble, self-effacing, self-sacrificing service of the Christian nurse she saw something of the miracle Isaac Watts describes in his well-known hymn:

> When I survey the wondrous cross
> On which the Prince of Glory died,
> My richest gain I count but loss
> And pour contempt on all my pride.
>
> Were the whole realm of nature mine,
> That were a tribute far too small;
> Love so amazing, so divine,
> Demands my soul, my life, my all.

Do You Put Your Money Where Your Heart Is?

A newspaper feature writer was given the assignment of writing a biographical series on the life of a prominent citizen recently deceased.

With characteristic thoroughness he searched out and examined every possible source of information. He read and marked dozens of addresses the man had delivered and also read the two books he had written.

He went through hundreds of the dead man's letters and conversed with many of his friends. He spent hours speaking with various members of the family. Although he had accumulated voluminous notes, he still felt that an essential "angle" was missing — something he could use as the motif of his entire series.

Finally one day the widow remarked: "I have a large box of my husband's check stubs in the attic. Would you like to look through them?"

He did. And there on hundreds of check stubs he discovered the inner soul of the man he could never quite fully understand.

In a very real sense it is what a man *gives to* that reveals most cleary what he is. Jesus once said: "Where your treasure is, there will your heart be also" (Matt. 6:21). We can also turn those words around and say: "Where your heart is, there will your treasure also be."

Our money has a way of going in the same direction as our thoughts. It has a way of gravitating toward those things which mean the most to us. The money of the heavy drinker has a way of ending up in the local tavern, while the money of the compulsive gambler rolls irresistibly into the coffers of the nearest race track.

On the other hand, he who through faith in Christ has given himself over to the service of the Lord and to the service of his fellowman will find himself giving of his earthly treasure for these selfsame purposes: the service of God and the service of man.

He will inevitably find himself putting his money where his heart is. The direction of his money will, in a very real sense, reveal the direction of his life.

Surely, every one of us has reason to heed the lesson of the check stubs. And in doing so we well might pray:

> Savior, Thy dying love
> Thou gavest me;
> Nor should I aught withhold,
> Dear Lord, from Thee.
> In love my soul would bow,
> My heart fulfill its vow,
> Some offering bring Thee now,
> Something for Thee.

"I Am the Way"

In Malaya, during the Second World War, a sympathetic native was helping an escaping prisoner of war make his way to the coast — and from there to freedom.

The two were stumbling through a virtually impenetrable jungle. There was no sign of human life and not even the slightest trace of a trail. Having grown weary and becoming somewhat wary, the soldier turned to his guide and asked: "Are you sure this is the way?"

The reply came in faltering English: "There *is* no way. . . . *I* am the way."

There was no beaten path to be followed, no trodden trail by which to guide their footsteps, no passage marked by those who had gone before. If the soldier was finally to reach the promised clearing, he had no alternative but to keep his eyes fixed steadily on the man who was befriending him and to follow wherever he might lead.

That was the meaning of the native's short reply: "There *is* no way. . . . *I* am the way."

Someone else said very much the same thing nearly two thousand years ago. It was the night before the Savior's crucifixion. Speaking to His despondent disciples about the glorious freedom that awaited them in His Father's house above, He said: "I am the Way." (John 14:6)

He not only *spoke* about the way to His Father's house, He not only *showed* the way, He *was* the Way! No matter what the future might hold for His faithful few who had gathered with Him on that fateful night (and for almost all of them the future held a martyr's death), if they would cling to *Him* in trusting faith, He would bring them safely home. He, and He alone, was the one sure Way.

And the same is true for you and me today. In a world of growing chaos and confusion, when old and familiar landmarks are gradually disappearing, when tried and trusted paths are becoming more and more obscured and life is taking on the aspects of the jungle, let us thank God that our hand is firmly in the hand of Him who has proved Himself "the Way."

By His life, by His death, and by His glorious resurrection He has shown Himself to be not only our Savior and Redeemer but also "the Son of God with power" (Rom. 1:14). Him we can trust. Him we can follow. To Him we can commit ourselves, body and soul, for time and eternity.

Now and forever He will be "the Way."

> Thou art the Way; to Thee alone
> From sin and death we flee;
> And He who would the Father seek
> Must seek Him, Lord, by Thee.

Is Yours a Cut-Flower Religion?

*T*here is something charming about cut flowers in a lovely vase. Properly arranged and interspersed with appropriate green they bring the fragrance, grace, and beauty of the garden into the living room or dining room.

And yet, although the cut flower stands proudly in the vase, there is no denying the fact that it is living on borrowed time. It began to die the minute its stem was snipped, and it will be only a matter of time, perhaps only hours, before its fragrant petals will begin to droop and wither and fall to the floor.

There is of course nothing overwhelmingly tragic about the drooping and wilting of a flower. There will always be another flower to take its place. But there *is* something overwhelmingly tragic about a social and spiritual phenomenon of our day, of which the wilting flower is but a striking symbol.

Recently a Stanford University professor, commenting on contemporary America, said: "The terrible danger of our time is the fact that ours is a cut-flower civilization. Beautiful as cut flowers may be . . . they will eventually die . . . because they have been severed from their roots.

"We are trying to maintain the dignity of the individual," he continued, "apart from the deep faith that every man is made in God's image and is therefore precious in God's eyes."

How tragically true! Many a person today, perhaps even many a church member, is trying desperately to demonstrate the fruits of true religion without having any vital contact

132

with the only Source of true religious faith and life. His is only a "cut-flower" religion, severed from the nourishing root and therefore without any real inner life and power.

Well might we heed the words of the Savior: "Abide in Me and I in you. As the branch cannot bear fruit of itself, except it abide in the vine, no more can ye, except ye abide in Me. I am the vine, ye are the branches. He that abideth in Me and I in him, the same bringeth forth much fruit; for without Me ye can do nothing." (John 15:4-5)

Abiding in Christ means maintaining daily, vital contact with Him through prayer, through Word, and Sacrament. It means maintaining intimate and *conscious* communion with Him throughout our waking hours. It means talking with Him, walking with Him, living with Him as we go about our daily tasks.

Are we really doing that? Are we really deriving the spiritual power for our Christian faith and life directly from the Source — from Him "who strengthens us"? (Phil. 4:13)

Or is ours a cut-flower religion?

She "Lost Her Steeple"

*L*ittle Joanne had completed her first month in kindergarten. Having said good-bye to her teacher at the close of day, she scampered down the corridor with her classmates and disappeared from sight.

A few minutes later she was back at her teacher's desk, her cheeks wet with tears. "I lost my steeple!" she sobbed. Puzzled and unable to understand the child's complaint, the teacher dried her tears and invited her to sit down and explain. At length she heard the following tearful story unfold:

On the first day of kindergarten Joanne's mother had pointed out a high church steeple just two blocks from the school. If Joanne would walk toward that steeple, she would be walking in the right direction. She would be walking toward her home.

But on this particular day Joanne had left the school by a different door, and as she looked up she found to her utter dismay that she had "lost her steeple" — and with no steeple by which to guide her footsteps she found herself in a world that was utterly strange.

Small wonder her little heart was frightened!

Is little Joanne perhaps a symbol of the world in which we live today? Could it be that many who are much older than Joanne have "lost their steeple" — that they have no sure, strong, enduring landmark by which to guide their pilgrim path on the journey home?

God has given you and me an immovable landmark

which, if we will but keep our eyes fixed steadily upon it, will enable us to thread our way through the increasing complexities of life.

The author of the Letter to the Hebrews put it this way: "Let us lay aside every weight, and the sin which doth so easily beset us, and let us run with patience the race that is set before us, *looking unto Jesus,* the Author and Finisher of our faith." (Heb. 12:1-2)

To the believer there is one enduring and unchanging landmark pointing the way on his journey home — "Jesus Christ, the same yesterday and today and forever." (Heb. 13:8)

Amid the crisscrossed highways and byways of life the believer can raise eyes of faith to Him who is his Lord and Savior. As long as he can see *Him,* he cannot be lost. As long as he looks toward Christ, the tangled pathways of life can hold no terror.

Little Joanne needed her steeple. The believer needs — and has — his Savior. And to Him he *looks.*

> I am trusting Thee to guide me;
>   Thou alone shalt lead,
> Every day and hour supplying
>   All my need.

"The Word Made Flesh"

$\mathcal{A}$ nuclear scientist was making an urgent plea for scholarships to be given to American students who would study in foreign lands. Stressing that such scholarships would win for America a much greater measure of understanding abroad, he said significantly: "The best way to send an idea out into the world is to wrap it up in a person."

In a sense infinitely more sublime, that is exactly what the Lord of heaven did on that first Christmas Eve. He had an "idea" which He was eager to convey to man, the message of His divine love, the word of pardon, peace, and joy. In His unsearchable wisdom He took this "idea," which He was so eager to communicate to the human family, wrapped it up in a person, and laid it into a manger.

That is the eternal significance of Christmas. "Without controversy, great is the mystery of godliness," says St. Paul. "God was manifest in the flesh" (1 Tim. 3:16). "The Word was made flesh," St. John tells us, "and dwelt among us, and we beheld His glory, the glory as of the Only-Begotten of the Father, full of grace and truth." (John 1:14)

Indeed, God wrapped up the wondrous message of His love in the Person of His only-begotten Son and sent that Son from heaven to earth, so that all men everywhere might know what is in His Father-heart: His good and gracious will toward all mankind, His mercy, His compassion.

That is why in spirit we kneel before the manger bed and greet the heavenly Visitor:

O Word of God Incarnate,
O Wisdom from on high,
O Truth unchanged, unchanging,
O Lord of our dark sky.

The Babe of Bethlehem is the Word of God Incarnate. He *is* the message of God to man. His holy birth, His sinless life, His atoning death, His triumphant resurrection, His glorious ascension — these we have beheld with the eyes of faith. These have revealed to us the love that is in the heart of the Father. These have revealed to us the open gate of heaven.

To all who seek to know what is in the heart of the God of heaven the Christmas Gospel extends the invitation: "Come to Bethlehem's manger. Here is the heart of God revealed. Here is *the Word of God made flesh.*"

"Not Here Long"

*T*he mailman studied the envelope as he made his way through the snow to the Flemming home. He had recognized the familiar return address in the upper left-hand corner.

It was the address of the Flemmings' son who was in an army camp in the South. He smiled as, beneath the young man's scribbled return address, he read the three words "Not here long."

It was the young man's way of telling his parents, almost as an afterthought, that he may not be at the same address the next time he would write.

As the mailman trudged through the snowbanks to the next house down the street, he mused: "Not here long. How appropriate those words would be under *any* return address!"

He had delivered mail in the same community for nearly 40 years, and many of those to whom he had brought letters in his early years were no longer among the living.

"Not here long." How true!

Especially at the close of the old year and the opening of the new the Christian is reminded that "here we have no continuing city" (Heb. 13:14). Here we have no permanent address. "But we seek one to come."

Or as Moses tells us in Psalm 90: "The years of our life are threescore and ten, or even by reason of strength fourscore; yet their span is but toil and trouble; they are soon gone, and we fly away."

How important that we cultivate a sense of the brevity of

life and the certainty of death! How much *more* important, however, that we live in the constant awareness of the things that are eternal!

If it be true that we are "not here long" — and surely it *is* true — we will want to spend our sojourn here as pilgrims whose eyes are on the homeland, "from whence we look for the Savior, the Lord Jesus Christ." (Phil. 3:20)

It is in *that* homeland that we hold our permanent citizenship.

In the Savior's Presence

*P*hillips Brooks was a noted American preacher of the 19th century. Highly respected by the general public because of his gifts as an orator, he was also well beloved by his intimate friends because of his winning, captivating personality.

One day a young college student who was deeply troubled by a spiritual problem gathered sufficient courage to ask this great man for a private interview. Happy to grant the young man's request, Brooks invited him into his study.

For more than an hour and a half the two engaged in serious conversation, the older man speaking with a depth of conviction and a sincerity of purpose that deeply impressed the younger.

Later that day the young man was asked by one of his classmates: "What did Dr. Brooks have to say about your problem?" To the astonishment of the classmate, the young man replied: "I never mentioned it. I was so captivated by his magnetic personality that my problem didn't seem important. It was enough for me just to have been with him — and to have listened."

How very much like the experience the devout believer frequently has with Jesus Christ, his Savior! To have been with Christ in an hour of quiet communion and to have *listened* is frequently the surest way to put all our personal problems into their proper perspective.

There is a power in the very person of Christ that has a way of softening our problems and solving our perplexities.

To spend a few minutes in His presence, to listen attentively to His Word, to submit to and *follow* the promptings of His Holy Spirit will bring more light and joy and confidence into our lives than a point-by-point rehearsal of all our personal problems.

Let us cultivate the daily habit of living consciously in the Savior's presence. The magnetic power of His divine personality as He speaks to our hearts through the words of Sacred Scripture will serve to put our many problems into their proper place.

Above all, He will speak peace to our souls, the peace the world cannot give, the peace He has won for us on Calvary's cross. Living in the light of that peace, all shadows will fall behind us.

> O Jesus, King most wonderful,
>   Thou Conqueror renowned,
> Thou Sweetness most ineffable,
>   In whom all joys are found!
>
> When once Thou visitest the heart,
>   Then truth begins to shine,
> Then earthly vanities depart,
>   Then kindles love divine.
>
> May every heart confess Thy name
>   And ever Thee adore;
> And, seeking Thee, itself inflame
>   To seek Thee more and more!
>
> Thee may our tongues forever bless,
>   Thee may we love alone,
> And ever in our lives express
>   The image of Thine own.

"Let Me Be!"

We had tuned into a religious service on our kitchen radio. After a few preliminary remarks the golden-voiced announcer informed his radio audience: "The first hymn to be sung by the congregation will be: 'Take My Life and Let It Be.'"

Our initial smile faded into an expression of thoughtful concern as we reflected on the tragic implications of that first line of the well-known hymn — if it is left to stand alone.

How many a person has come to the Lord with the selfish prayer: "Take my life and let it *be!*" Take my life into Thy safekeeping, O Lord, but after that please do not disturb me. Please, let me *be!*

Such was not the mind of the great apostle. He knew that once his life had been taken over by his Lord, his life was no longer his. He was perfectly willing to turn the reins over to Him who was both his Lord and Savior.

He tells his Philippian Christians: "I press on, hoping to take hold of that for which Christ once took hold of me" (Phil. 3:12 NEB). Christ had indeed taken hold of Paul. Now Paul's supreme desire was to take hold of the things for which Christ had called him. Christ had called him not into retirement but into action.

He expresses the same thought, but in different language, to the believers in Galatia: "The life I now live is not *my* life but the life which Christ lives in me; and my present bodily life is lived by faith in the Son of God, who loved me and sacrificed Himself for me." (Gal. 2:20 NEB)

Christ had indeed taken Paul's life. But in its stead He had given him something far more precious: the life of faith and love and joy and humble service.

Christ has done the same for you and me. He has taken our lives and given us His. He wills to live *within* us. He wills that our lips, our hands, our feet carry out His high and holy purpose — in loving service to our fellowmen.

No, Christ never takes a life to "let it be." He takes our lives to use them, to enlist them, to enable them for service in His kingdom.

Let our daily prayer, then, be the entire stanza of the well known hymn:

> Take my life and let it be
> Consecrated, Lord, to Thee;
> Take my moments and my days,
> Let them flow in ceaseless praise.

God's Little Whiles

*L*ittle Tommy lay seriously ill in his hospital bed. A smiling nurse entered his room. Interpreting his somber mood as a sign of loneliness or fear, she remarked conversationally: "Didn't I see your mother in here before?"

At the sound of the word "mother" there was a flicker of light in the lad's feverish eyes, as if suddenly he had made contact with a brand new source of strength.

Raising his head ever so slightly, he assured the nurse, with a burst of energy that taxed his fevered frame: "She's coming back! She said she'd only be gone a *little while*."

With a knowing smile the understanding nurse patted his head and went about her duties. She knew that the magic of the promised "little while" would buoy his spirits until he saw his mother's face again.

Have *we* learned the secret of living by "little whiles"? *God's* little whiles? The Savior once told His sorrowing disciples: "A little while and ye shall not see Me; and again a little while and ye shall see Me. . . . Ye shall be sorrowful, but your sorrow shall be turned into joy." (John 16:16, 20)

In a sense the life of the Christian is a constant succession of many of God's little whiles. Our Lord sometimes sends us sorrow, but our sorrows are separated from our joys by only "little whiles." "For a small moment I have forsaken thee," He says, "but with great mercies will I gather thee" (Is. 54:7). And again: "Weeping may endure for the night, but joy cometh in the morning." (Ps. 30:5)

144

Life itself is but a "little while" in the calendar of God's eternity. Life's little while, the Bible assures us, will soon be swallowed up in the endless ages of pure delight in heaven.

Lazarus spent a "little while" begging crumbs at the gate of the rich man's palace, but he is spending an eternity of bliss in Abraham's bosom. The malefactor spent a "little while" suspended on the cross, but his sorrow was soon turned into the endless joy of Paradise.

Matching our *little* whiles of sadness with our *big* whiles of gladness, the apostle Paul reminds us: "The sufferings of this present time are not worthy to be compared with the glory which shall be revealed in us." (Rom. 8:18)

The Christian accepts his little whiles of pain and sorrow as preludes to a perfect day. He knows that his sorrow will be turned into joy; his shadows into sunshine; his little whiles of doubt and trial, of loneliness and fear into eternal ages of joy and glory in the company of heaven.

He knows that beyond each frowning "little while" there is the radiant face of One who loves him and who, like little Tommy's mother, has promised to "come back."

"All We Need"

*M*any years ago in Scotland there was a faithful Christian pastor who followed a splendid custom. Every year on a certain Sunday he would preach a sermon on the theme "Jesus, the Lamb of God."

So consistent had this habit become that some of the elder members of his congregation had affectionately named this particular date on the calendar "Lamb of God Sunday."

On the Sabbath morning before he died he was too weak to enter his pulpit. Seated in a chair, he spoke to his congregation on his favorite theme. Despite the protests of his family, he occupied the same chair for the *evening* service — and again he spoke on the theme that had endeared him to his faithful flock.

When he returned to his study later that evening, his daughter asked him: "Father, why didn't you choose a different text for your sermon this evening?" Without hesitation he replied: "My daughter, that is all they need — the Lamb of God, which taketh away the sin of the world."

Living in the very shadow of *death,* the old man could see more clearly than ever what was the primary need of life: a personal faith in the sin-atoning Savior. "That is all they need," he said.

Can the same be said today? In a society that is becoming more and more complex, in which our personal problems seem to be growing more and more involved and our personal "needs" seem to be multiplying day after day, can it still be said: "That is all they *need*"?

In a very real sense, yes! Our greatest need, beside which all others fade into relative insignificance, is a filial son-or-daughter relationship to our heavenly Father. To know beyond doubt that we are His, that He is ours, that nothing in life or death can ever separate us — what greater need could mortal man experience?

And that need has been met for us in "the Lamb of God, which taketh away the sin of the world." It is in His birth, life, death, and resurrection that our deepest fears are stilled and our highest hopes find full fruition.

It was of this heaven-sent Savior that the poet wrote those words so precious to the heart of the believer: "Thou, O Christ, art all I want; More than all in Thee I find."

What a comfort, as we face the duties of each new day and as we close our eyes in sleep each night, to know that in the Christ of the manger and the Christ of the cross we indeed have "all we need"!

> Lamb of God, we fall before Thee,
>   Humbly trusting in Thy cross.
> That alone be all our glory;
>   All things else are only dross.
>
> Thee we own a perfect Savior,
>   Only Source of all that's good.
> Every grace and every favor
>   Comes to us through Jesus' blood.

He Loved Them to the End

A young man who had been away from home for several years received word that his father was critically ill.

Guilt-stricken because he had not written to his father in months, he boarded the first plane and hurried home. He was determined, at this late moment, to make up for his neglect and to assure the dying man of his filial affection.

To his dismay he arrived just an hour too late. The angel of death had deprived him of that precious moment of reunion he had craved so earnestly. It was a crushed young man who watered his pillow with tears that night. If only he could know how his father felt toward him in his dying moments!

The next morning his sister handed him a letter his father had written him a few days before but which had never been mailed. Tears filled the young man's eyes as he eagerly read each line. His father bore him no ill will. He still loved him, as he had down through the years. The letter was signed "With *love*. Your Father."

In the Gospel of St. John is a sentence that should affect us very much the same as the dying father's letter affected his guilt-stricken son. Near the opening of the Lenten story the evangelist tells us of Jesus: "Having loved His own, He loved them unto the end." (John 13:1)

If any guilt-ridden sinner needs the reassurance of His heavenly Father's tender mercy, let him read our Savior's love letter in the 'teen chapters of St. John. Standing under the very shadow of the cross, knowing that He would soon lay down

His life for the sins of the world, the Redeemer is at great pains to assure us of His dying love.

"As My Father hath loved me, so have I loved you. Continue ye in My love. . . . Greater love hath no man than this, that a man lay down His life for His friends. . . . The Father Himself loveth you, because ye have loved Me and have believed that I came out from God." (John 15:9, 13; 16:27)

It should be a source of endless comfort to us that on the night before His crucifixion, with the agonies of Gethsemane and Calvary only a matter of hours away, our Savior sought again and again to assure us of His love. And having done His best to assure us, He walked resolutely into the jaws of death — to give us life.

"Having loved His own, He loved them unto the end."

> His love, what mortal thought can reach!
> What mortal tongue display!
> Imagination's utmost stretch
> In wonder dies away.
>
> Dear Lord, while we our praises sing
> And grateful voices blend,
> May every heart with rapture sing:
> "He loved me to the end!"

Thou, God, Seest Me

A little boy visiting in the home of an elderly woman was intrigued by a colored wall motto bearing the Biblical text: "Thou, God, seest me." Noticing the child's interest, the kindly woman took the motto from the wall and began explaining it to the lad.

"Some people will tell you," she said, "that God is always watching to see when you are doing wrong — so He can punish you.

"I don't want you to think of this motto in that way. Every time you read the words, 'Thou, God, seest me,' I would rather have you remember that God loves you so much that *He cannot take His eyes off you.*"

How correct she was! Martin Luther would have declared this woman a doctor of divinity, for she had learned how to tell Law from Gospel. To the wicked and impenitent there is indeed the threat of punishment in the thought, "Thou, God, seest me." But to the believer in Christ there is nothing but sweet assurance in those words.

Again and again the Scriptures tell us that the eyes of the Lord are upon those that are His. David tells us: "The eyes of the Lord are upon the righteous, and His ears are open unto their cry" (Ps. 34:15). As the loving mother cannot take her eyes off her newborn child, so the Lord "withdraweth not His eyes" from those who put their trust in Him (Job 36:7). They are always the objects of His tender care.

To the person who has been made a child of God through

faith in Christ, there is comfort in the thought that every hour of the day and night he is in the heavenly Father's eye. He knows that, through Christ, the eyes of God have become the eyes of love and tender mercy.

To the believer in Christ the motto "Thou, God, seest me" is as much a prayer of gratitude as it is an expression of trust and confident assurance. What permanent harm can befall him if his Father's eyes are constantly upon him?

It would be difficult to improve on the explanation the elderly woman gave to her little visitor: "Every time you read these words, 'Thou, God, seest me,' I would rather have you remember that God loves you so much that *He cannot take His eyes off you.*"

Writing Checks on God's Promises

*I*t happened at a banquet given in honor of Hollywood notables.

A successful producer was seated next to the wealthy widow of a movie executive. During the course of their dinner conversation he alluded briefly to certain of his religious convictions.

Surprised, his dinner companion asked him very pointedly: "Do you really believe there is a God?"

Taken somewhat aback, the producer was momentarily at a loss for an answer. But after a brief moment he replied:

"You are a wealthy woman. Are you not?"

To which she nodded her assent.

"How do you know you are wealthy? Have you ever really *seen* your wealth? I doubt very much that you have. But you know you are a woman of great material resources because you can write checks in large amounts, and they are always honored."

And then he concluded: "I've never seen God. But I've been writing checks on His promises for many years, and they've always been honored. So, if you ask me if I believe there is a God, my only answer can be — yes."

The believer in Christ is, in a very real sense, writing checks on God's promises every day of his life. Because he has become God's child through faith in the Redeemer, he has fallen heir to an inexhaustible spiritual treasure — set aside for him "in the heavenlies."

Again and again in his epistles St. Paul refers to the "riches" which God has, as it were, earmarked and made available to those who come to Him in the name of His Son.

He tells the Ephesian Christians that he never ceases to pray "that you may receive that inner illumination of the spirit which will make you realize how great is the hope to which God is calling — the magnificence and splendor of the inheritance promised to Christians — and how tremendous is the power available to us who believe in God." (Eph. 1:18-19 Phillips)

He assures his Philippians: "My God will supply all that you need from His glorious resources in Christ Jesus" (Phil. 4:19 Phillips). This is the same God of whom he says in another place that He "is able to do far more than we ever dare to ask or imagine." (Eph. 3:20 Phillips)

Forgiveness of sins, life, and salvation — these are the eternal and inexhaustible riches God has written to the credit of all who trust His sin-atoning Son. These are the unspeakable riches on which you and I can "write checks" each day of our lives. We have *His* word for it.

"As to the Lord"

A scrubwoman was once approached by an active church member and asked: "And what work do *you* do for the Lord?"

Her reply was simple and direct. *"All of it,"* she said.

There was perhaps more good theology in those three words than in any other answer the woman could have given.

All of her work was being done for the Lord!

While it was no doubt true that some of her deeds were more directly in the service of the Lord than others, she nevertheless felt that *everything* she did was in the service of her Master.

There is a lesson for all of us in the simple answer of this humble woman.

In a day that is inclined to draw too sharp a line between the sacred and the secular, there is an ever-present danger that we draw an artificial distinction between what we do for the Lord through the organizational channels of the church and what we do for Him in the humdrum routine of our everyday life.

The dead-tired young mother walking the floor with her sick child at night, the harried young father working long hours to make a living for his wife and children, the laborer at his bench, the student at his desk, the secretary at her typewriter, the pilot at the controls of his plane — all can be performing their respective duties "as to the Lord."

The apostle Paul tells us: *"Whatsoever* ye do [whatever

our station in life demands of us in the way of daily routine], do it heartily, as to the Lord, and not unto men . . . for ye serve the Lord Christ." (Col. 3:23-24)

The Christian serves his Lord Christ in every station of life: as father, mother, son, daughter, employer, employee, teacher, student, executive, or — scrubwoman. *Whatever* his calling, if it be to the glory of God and the welfare of his fellowman, he can discharge his daily duties "as to the Lord."

Let us beware of too sharp a distinction between the sacred and the secular. To the Christian *all* things are sacred. He has dedicated them all to the service of the Most High.

That is what the humble scrubwoman meant when she replied to the question: "And what work do *you* do for the Lord?" by saying: "All of it!" There was nothing that she was not doing for Him.

Can we say the same?

Pilgrims, Transients, Wayfarers

---

*T*he story is told of a wayfarer who many years ago knocked on the door of a medieval English castle.

"Please, sir, may I have lodging for the night?" he asked the stout man who answered the knock.

"This castle is not for pilgrims," the grim-faced man replied as he made a move to close the door.

"Are you the owner, sir?" the wayfarer inquired.

"I am."

"And who lived in this castle before you?"

"My father."

"And who will live in it when you are gone?"

"My son."

"And still you say, sir, this castle is not for *pilgrims?*"

The believer in Christ needs to be reminded from time to time that in this world he is indeed a pilgrim. Perhaps at no time are we more aware of our pilgrim role than at the closing of each year, when we take a look back over the path we have traveled and spend an hour in quiet meditation.

We are, all of us, wayfarers on a distant road, far from our Father's house. In the words of Scripture, "Here have we no continuing city, but we seek one to come" (Heb. 13:14). We are foreigners traveling through a strange land — with the light of the homeland in our eyes!

As we sit alone with our December thoughts, contemplating the imminent death of another year, our hearts are attuned to the psalmist's: "As for man, his days are as grass; as a flower of the field, so he flourisheth. For the wind passeth over it, and it is gone; and the place thereof shall know it no more."

But we also hasten to add with the psalmist: "But the mercy of the Lord is from everlasting to everlasting upon them that fear Him, and His righteousness unto children's children." (Ps. 103:17)

Pilgrims, transients, wayfarers in a distant country, but children of a gracious Father and brothers of our Savior Christ! At the turning of another year we look back on the far stretch we have traveled and then look forward to the shortening path that lies ahead.

And with the eyes of faith we see — in the unmeasured distance — the lighted windows of our Father's house.

> One sweetly solemn thought
>   Comes to me o'er and o'er:
> Nearer my home today am I
>   Than e'er I've been before.
>
> Nearer my Father's house,
>   Where many mansions be;
> Nearer today the great white throne,
>   Nearer the crystal sea.

"If Not Here — *There*"

*O*ur sleek silver jet had just thundered down the runway of the Los Angeles airport. Gracefully it headed out over the Pacific, made its usual half-circle turn, and then headed eastward across the continent below.

Worn and weary after six hectic weeks in the movie capital, we sat back in our seat and, as is our custom at the start of each new flight, breathed a silent prayer.

"Lord, bring me safely home," we prayed. And then, looking out into the infinity of blue beyond our window, we added quietly: "If not here — *there*."

That was all we prayed. But somehow the echo of that brief petition stayed with us every moment of our flight. The assurance that our heavenly Father would answer it according to His gracious will rested upon us as a heavenly benediction — as we crossed soaring mountains and verdant valleys and sun-parched prairies at almost the speed of sound.

"Lord, bring me safely home. If not here — *there*." Isn't this, in its simplest terms, the prayer of every believer in Christ as he ventures forth on the unknown path of each new day? After the toil and the sweat, the noise and the turmoil of each of life's little days he knows that the Lord will bring him safely home to the company of loved ones, either here or there.

And he knows this, not because of the shallow assurance of some sentimental greeting card but because he bears in his heart the Spirit-wrought conviction that the Lord of heaven has intervened in his behalf. The God of the trackless universe, through the redeeming work of His beloved Son, has assured him of a home that is open and waiting — *there.*

It was His divine Son who said: "In My Father's house are many mansions. . . . I go to prepare a place for you . . . that where I am, there ye may be also" (John 14:2-3). It was the apostle Paul who brought comfort and strength to the early Christians with the reminder: "Our conversation [our homeland] is in heaven, from whence also we look for the Savior, the Lord Jesus Christ." (Phil. 3:20)

To the Christian pilgrim who has caught the heavenly vision, his earthly dwelling can never be more than his "home away from home." His permanent and abiding dwelling place is now and always in the mansions of his Father.

And so, at the dawn of each new day, as we set our feet on the untrod path before us, we can pray with quiet confidence: "Lord, bring me safely home. If not here — *there.* Through Jesus Christ, my Lord."

Topical Index